ABOU

PETER LIGHTBO... ... ...,
England and moved to Australia with his family
in 1960. His love affair with golf began at the
age of 12. A short and boring stint in the Public
Service convinced him to turn professional,
which he did in 1972. He has taught extensively
in Australia, and in London, Denmark and
Malta. He is now teaching professional at
Macquarie University Golf Driving Range in
Sydney.

CECILIA CROAKER was born in Sydney and
studied literature and languages at the
University of Sydney, and later librarianship at
the University of NSW. After working in
libraries and bookshops and travelling, she is
now a writer and mother.

Cecilia and Peter are married with one son
and a black and white cat.

THE ART OF GOLF

A Guide to Playing through Self-Awareness

Peter Lightbown
and
Cecilia Croaker

ACKNOWLEDGMENTS

Dedicated to Ron Farmer with our thanks.

Our thanks also to photographers Paul Richardson, Philip Barling, Simon Freeman and Kristina Poder, and to New South Wales and Wakehurst Golf Clubs for permission to use their courses.

Published by ABC Books for the
AUSTRALIAN BROADCASTING CORPORATION
GPO Box 9994 Sydney NSW 2001

First published August, 1995

National Library of Australia
Cataloguing-in-Publication entry
Lightbown, Peter.
 The art of golf: a guide to playing through
 self-awareness.
 Includes index.
 ISBN 0 7333 0466 4.
 1. Golf. 2. Golf – Psychological aspects.
 3. Self-perception. I. Croaker, Cecilia. II. Australian
 Broadcasting Corporation. III. Title.
796.352

Designed by Geoff Morrison

Front Cover photographs: Live Action/

Set in 11 on 14 point Bembo by Keyset, Sydney

Printed and bound in Australia by Southwood Press, Marrickville.

1495-7

5 4 3 2 1

Contents

Foreword

There have been many many books produced on the technique of golf, and I expect there will be countless more. It suggests of course that golf playing is more a science than a sport.

It wasn't always so. Golf began spontaneously somewhere back in the mists of time along the links of Scotland. In Man it seems is a basic compulsion to strike at round objects with the aim of sending them on their way. The activity is intriguing enough to be called a game.

Eventually there were Rules made to administer contests, and finally in its evolution, scoring was invented. Thus the game progressed for some hundreds of years before technique reared its head.

Today though, there are thousands of addicted persons who would dearly love to play better, or at least eliminate the woeful shots that cause embarrassment and irritation. It is to this vast army that instruction manuals aim their message.

Personally, I have always been afraid of messages on technique because my early tastes of such left a distinct flavour of acid. I carefully threaded my way through the minefield like a man with a metal detector.

Having now ended my search for perfection, I can happily open my mind to matters of technique, observing as I have that with all the modern methods of teaching and training there is scant improvement, if any, in the way people play their golf.

It seems to me that if the recent plethora of advice was of any real value, our modern players would be showing us far and away better performances. I have a suspicion that most modern training guides are either on the wrong track or are hopeless at conveying their ideas.

I therefore read this manuscript with interest, and found much to my way of thinking. In the putting section, for example, I found for the first time in print what everyone from Harry Vardon down through Bobby Locke knew as basic — the putt is just a simple diminution of the full drive, so that the body has to do in miniature what it does to the fullest from the tee.

There are other gems too. But what I endorse most is the notion that golf is best played simply with natural instinctive movements befitting one's physique and strength.

If like me you want golf demystified and simplified, I reckon you will find much contained here of special interest. If it clears away the fog of technical jargon it will have served a fine purpose. Go to it!

Peter Thomson CBE

Introduction

How does the Meadow-flower its bloom unfold?
Because the lovely little flower is free
Down to its roots, and, in that freedom bold;
And so the grandeur of the Forest-tree
Comes not from its casting in a formal mould,
But from its own divine vitality.

WORDSWORTH

THE INSPIRATION FOR this book lies in my belief that within each one of us is a natural golf swing waiting to flower, a spontaneous movement with a freedom and vitality of its own. In my experience it is only when this individual and expressive movement starts to emerge that playing golf becomes satisfying and truly pleasurable. Unfortunately traditional golf teaching has denied our individuality and spontaneity by insisting that in order to learn we must conform rigidly to a pattern. The swing is thus broken up into a series of complicated operations which we are required to copy. In attempting to perform all the steps correctly our swing becomes something to be controlled and worried about, and the joy that can be found in a free use of the body is entirely lost to us.

Since the traditional method is so destructive of individuality and pleasure, I am advocating here a fundamentally different approach, one which seeks to draw out an innate swing that is unique to you. Such a movement by its very nature can never be copied or constructed, rather we must focus our attention entirely on creating the best possible conditions for its emergence. In the same way living things, be they animal or vegetable, cannot be made to grow, all we can do is use our knowledge to create an environment that fosters growth.

What then are the most favourable conditions for the growth of your swing? In my experience they are the qualities of balance, relaxation and rhythm, which I feel are the basic foundations on which all effective movement is built. As we will see later in more detail, balance is vital because it gives us the stability and security from which to move freely; relaxation is essential since it removes unnecessary tension, thus allowing us to release the full power of our muscles; rhythm plays the crucial role of blending or connecting movement into a coordinated powerful whole. As you learn to weave these qualities into the fabric of your movements a free and natural swing will of its own accord unfold.

Since balance, relaxation and rhythm are bodily feelings, we can never learn them by rote but need to perceive them actively through our senses. My principal task is to help increase your awareness of these vital qualities in your own body so that you experience them with ever more subtlety. It will take time and disciplined work to gain the sensitivity required but a greater bodily awareness is well within the scope of us all.

I came to these ideas because after fifteen years of constant work on traditional technique I arrived at a point of total frustration. For me golf had ceased to be a pleasurable activity and had instead become an arduous struggle to perform all the movements correctly. I realised that I had to either give up the game or find a more satisfying approach. It occurred to me about this time that the most accomplished players, while differing in many respects, all had three qualities in common — those of balance, relaxation and rhythm. Thus I began to work on introducing these qualities into my game rather than trying to construct a perfect technique. There was no instant transition. My game was littered for some time with mechanical considerations, but I gradually became aware of what it feels like to be really balanced and relaxed, and to have my movements flowing to the natural rhythm of my body. You could say that the game went from being predominantly external or mechanical to being internal or something of feeling. I have been using this approach and teaching it now for ten years and the results both in my own game and in those of my pupils are most encouraging.

I must emphasise at this point that I am not advocating the total abandonment of all technique. In my approach, however, technique exists solely in the service of the qualities we wish to foster and not for its own sake. So rather than giving you a collection of arbitrary do's and dont's to follow, I will be describing in detail practical ways of introducing balance, relaxation and rhythm into your game. This is in no way a soft or passive option since it requires you to give your complete attention to experiencing something for yourself. One might therefore describe this method as an active process of self-discovery, whereas the traditional method, which hinges on doing what one is told, could be described as profoundly passive.

Golfers of all levels will find this approach helpful, from advanced players who can subtly improve their game by becoming more sensitive to the qualities I recommend, to the beginner who has never played before. I realise that the beginner, and in particular a person with little or no sporting background, may find it difficult to believe that they have an individual swing to be uncovered. I can fully understand this situation because as a youth I felt myself to be something of a sporting outcast. However from my own experience as a player and as a teacher I can assure you that we all do have natural potential. It may show itself only rarely or perhaps not at all, but the fact that it is not on the surface does not mean that it does not exist. This is not to say that we all have equal amounts of natural ability, because some people are obviously more at home in a sporting environment than others. But I do feel that we limit ourselves more than necessary, in many cases by believing the restricted view of ourselves and our potential with which parents and teachers have saddled us. A step forward in any field is always a step into the unknown which requires us to take courage and have faith in ourselves and our unseen potential. If we can conceive of the possibility of our own growth we can in my view by our own efforts help to make it come true.

Let us now look at the qualities of balance, relaxation and rhythm in more detail.

1

Balance, Relaxation & Rhythm

I<small>T</small> <small>WILL BE USEFUL</small> to begin our exploration of balance, relaxation and rhythm by understanding what these qualities are and why they are so essential to our game.

Good balance can be defined as the stability we gain when our weight is evenly distributed. When we are well balanced we feel poised and steady. This is not a static quality since we are always making slight, hardly perceptible adjustments in order to finely balance our body. Even while standing 'still', for example, we are actually continually moving — minutely adjusting the distribution of our weight to maintain equilibrium. To understand what I mean you might like to try this simple experiment. Assume a normal standing position, close your eyes and just notice the extent to which your body moves. You may be surprised to find that standing 'still' is not still at all.

When our body is efficiently balanced these adjustments or oscillations are relatively small, whereas when we are poorly balanced they are quite large. The more we are able to efficiently balance the body and thus reduce its oscillations, the greater will be our solidity and feeling of security. In a golf stance this stability gives us the physical capacity and the confidence to move freely, and thus uninhibitedly release the full power of the swing *(pic 1)*. By contrast, when we are poorly balanced it is impossible to swing freely because it is difficult for our body to maintain itself in a state of equilibrium. As a result our swing becomes inhibited and defensive.

To be relaxed is to be free from unnecessary tension. This does not mean that our body is collapsed or floppy since a certain amount of muscle tension is necessary to stand upright or do any work, but rather that our muscles are in an optimum state of tension and not over-tightened.

Relaxation is vitally important in a golf swing for two reasons. Firstly it promotes ease of movement by freeing our muscles to function effectively. Relaxed muscles are charged with energy and ready to work, whereas over-tensed ones are inhibited in their ability to sustain movement since they are already holding excessive tension and so are unable to handle an increased workload.

The other key advantage of relaxation is that it increases our awareness of our body. This is essential because playing golf, like any skillful activity, depends on us being able to feel what we are doing with great delicacy. Tension, on the other hand, cuts off feeling and restricts the feedback we get from our body. For instance most people grip the club so tightly that they are unable to feel the clubhead with sufficient sensitivity. A relaxed 'grip' will greatly increase our awareness of the clubhead and so allow us to use it with delicacy and precision.

The principal problem we encounter when learning to relax is that we are in fact often totally unaware of the excessive tension we are holding. This is because tension has become part of the way we habitually do things and so seems normal and even comfortable to us. You may have experienced, for example, that it is only after a few weeks of relaxation on holiday that you realize just how tense you usually are. Thus

1 Good balance gives us the poise and steadiness so characteristic of a powerful swing.

in order to introduce relaxation into your golf swing I will begin by helping you to recognise the level of unnecessary tension you unconsciously hold, and then show you effective ways of dissipating it.

Rhythm is a natural pulse or beat that is found in our movements when they are free-flowing and spontaneous. It is a connecting, harmonising force which links movement together into a coordinated whole. In a rhythmic golf swing our body parts move as one to the beat of this internal pulse. In the absence of rhythm, movement ceases to flow freely and the swing becomes disjointed and jerky.

There are three principal advantages to rhythmic movement. Firstly, when all parts of the body are working harmoniously together rather than at odds with each other, the swing becomes extremely powerful. This is not power with effort but easeful, seemingly effortless power, since the stress and strain of trying have been replaced by the rhythmic flow of the body.

Secondly, a rhythmic swing has a regular predictable pattern. This makes it easy to judge how much power will be gained from each club and as a result we become much more confident in our club selection. By contrast, since unrhythmic movement is jerky it is unpredictable, making it impossible to judge the likely result of any shot.

Last but by no means least, it is a highly pleasurable and exhilarating experience to move uninhibitedly to the spontaneous rhythm of the body.

Since rhythm is by its very nature instinctive, we cannot consciously contrive or create it nor produce it by an act of will. Rather we will be looking at ways of unearthing this natural beat and learning to place our trust in it. As you become increasingly able to move to your innate rhythm, golf ceases to be an arduous struggle and you will find that the swing starts to swing you.

Balance, relaxation and rhythm are not, however, separate

entities but are inextricably linked. Each aids the other and all three need to be present together for the swing to be truly effective. For example, if excessive tension is held in one part of the body it will block the flow of movement and destroy the natural rhythm of the swing. If we are poorly balanced our body is fighting to maintain itself in a state of equilibrium and we inevitably become tense. When we are out of tune with the rhythm of the body, movement cannot flow freely so we have to 'make' things happen. The swing thus revolves around effort or force, in other words around tension.

By contrast, good balance is relaxing and frees the body to move uninhibitedly. Relaxation opens the way for spontaneous flowing movement, and rhythm is by its very nature effortless and therefore relaxing.

Let us now look in detail at practical ways of introducing these three interdependent qualities into every aspect of your game.

2

The

Stance

THE STANCE IS THE first area in which we need to create favourable conditions for the emergence of free and expressive movement. One might describe it as the basis on which everything else is built since a tense and poorly balanced stance can only produce a swing that echoes these defects. Once the body is balanced and relaxed in the stance, many swings are transformed instantly.

POSTURE

In my view the stance itself has its origin in our everyday standing posture, since the imbalance and tension present in our normal posture will automatically carry over into our golf stance. As an extreme example, the hunchback of Notre Dame would have undoubtedly transferred his posture to a golf stance, and what might have been tolerable for bell ringing would have had horrendous consequences as far as golf is concerned!

I must emphasise at this point that good posture has nothing whatsoever to do with 'standing up straight' as the military would understand this phrase. Such an approach would involve using the will to force the body into a state of upright immobility. In fact I do not see good posture in static terms at all but rather as a balanced and relaxed use of the body.

As children the vast majority of us started out with good posture, as any observation of small infants will show *(pic 2)*. However factors such as bending over school desks and later the awkwardness of adolescence have helped many of us lose the perfect posture we enjoyed when young. In order to retrace our steps we need to begin by understanding the two principal ways in which good posture is lost.

The Alignment of the Head

If you habitually carry your head dropped forward and down it causes the back to curve and the shoulders to become rounded, creating tension in both areas *(pic 3)*. As you will see later, this position seriously blocks a free movement of the upper half of the body in the swing.

The Position of the Pelvis

Many people, including myself at one time, habitually carry themselves in what might be described as a 'tail out' position. The pelvis is angled so that the upper edge pushes the stomach forward and the lower edge is pulled back. The knees are locked back with weight centralised on the heels *(pic 4)*. This whole position creates tension in the legs, slackness in the stomach muscles, and exaggerates the curve of the lower back causing tightness in that area. When this common approach to posture is transferred to a golf stance there is little likelihood of a free and active use of the lower half of the body in the swing. In fact adopting the stance itself becomes difficult since we are starting from a locked and frozen position and will therefore find it hard to effectively release our hip joint — perhaps the most essential element in a good stance.

We now need to look at ways of improving our posture, by encouraging a balanced, symmetrical placement of the head and by relaxing and realigning the pelvic area.

2 A typical four year old, with naturally perfect posture.

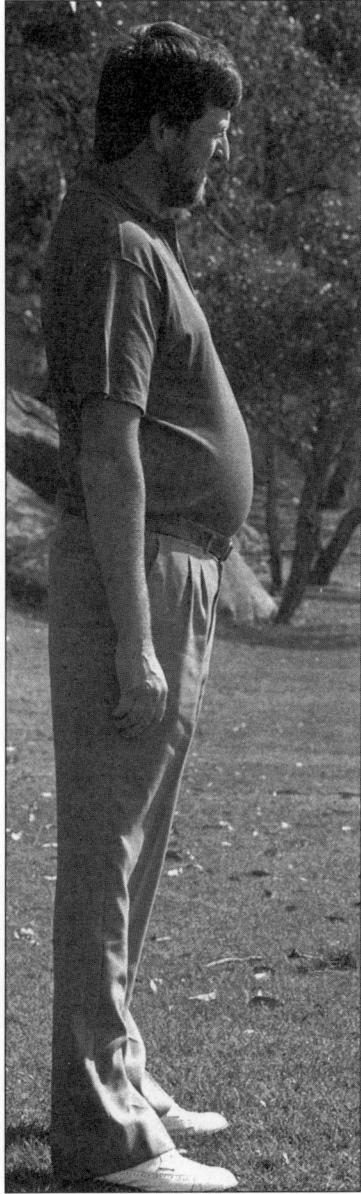

3 This is an exaggeration of a very common tendency. The position of the head has caused the whole body to 'collapse'. Notice the lack of tone in the stomach muscles.
4 The classic Australian 'beer-gut' position. Notice the angle of the belt and the locked tenseness of the legs.

The head

The following exercise is designed to improve the position of your head and in this way draw your spine out to its full length, thus reducing tension in the upper torso.

(i) Bend over double with your head hanging down, knees slightly bent, and your eyes closed *(pic 5a)*.

(ii) Become aware of the weight of your head as it hangs loosely from your neck.

(iii) Come up as slowly as possible, starting from the bottom of your spine. Imagine that you are gradually building yourself up vertebra by vertebra like a tower of children's wooden blocks. When you get to the point where your head is hanging from your upright torso, stop and then proceed even more slowly in the final section *(pic 5b)*.

(iv) Imagine that your head is a balloon which is gradually floating up as you slowly build the top seven vertebrae that make up the neck.

(v) Now focus on your shoulders, and as you breathe out deeply let all the tension drain away so that they drop slightly. Feel the weight of your arms hanging loosely at your sides *(pic 5c)*.

This exercise not only helps to free the spine but also promotes a feeling of lightness and well-being.

The pelvic position

The pelvic muscles are in essence the source of all powerful movement since they are the body's strongest muscles. In order to use these muscles effectively we need to free the pelvic area from unnecessary tension, and the following exercise is designed to do this.

(i) Flex your knees slightly and take your attention to your buttock muscles. Contract these muscles as much as you can,

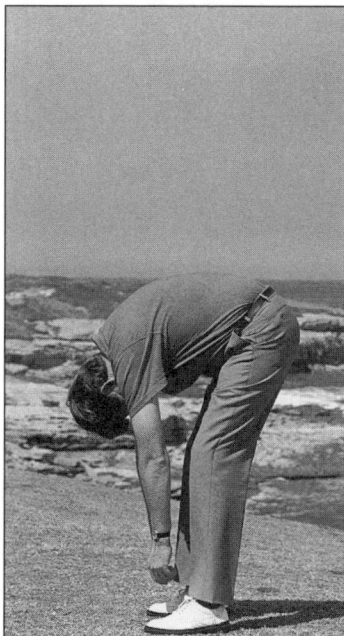

5a Bend and flop, letting all tension fall from the arms.
5b Let the head drop, with the chin practically touching the chest.
5c Imagine your head floating up like a balloon. You may feel several inches taller after doing this exercise.

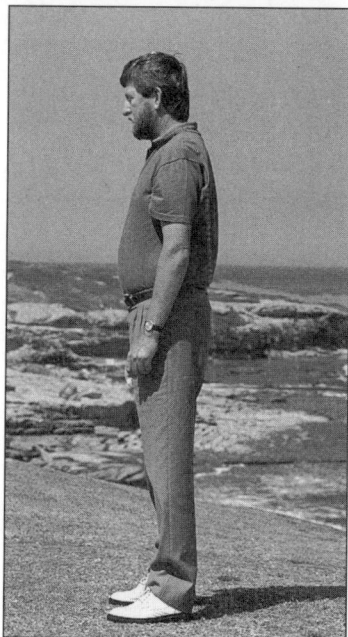

the tighter the better, and then release that tension completely, breathing out as you imagine the tension dropping away.

(ii) Place your hands either side of the pelvis, one on the buttocks and one on the lower abdomen, and gently tilt the lower edge of the pelvis under so that your genitals are carried forward *(pic 6)*. This should not be a violent movement, the slower and gentler the better.

(iii) When you have tilted the pelvis, again breathe out deeply and let tension drop away from this whole area of the body. We do not want the pelvis to be held in a new position by force, but rather allowed to find its natural position by removing tension from the muscles that surround it.

(iv) Check that your knees are still flexed and that weight is not concentrated on your heels but is spread evenly across the soles of your feet.

This exercise promotes a light and springy feeling in the legs and feet, freedom and mobility

6 When the pelvis is correctly tilted your belt will be parallel to the ground.

in the pelvis and good tone in the stomach muscles.

In order to fundamentally improve our posture, however, we must do more than practise these exercises occasionally. What is needed is an increasing awareness of the way in which we use our body in everyday situations. In my view it is impossible to spend our weekdays in a tense and twisted posture and then become magically relaxed on Saturday ready for a weekend of golf. So learn to observe the way in which you use your body in day-to-day activities. Take note of your head position as you walk down the street, and when standing check to see whether your knees are locked and your pelvis is angled back. As you notice your shortcomings in these areas, gently but persistently correct your posture. By doing this you will gradually learn to use your body in the most relaxed and efficient way possible.

The importance of good posture cannot be over-emphasised since it is the foundation on which a sound swing is built. Tension and imbalance in our posture inevitably filter through and inhibit freedom of movement in our swing. So posture cannot be dismissed as an irrelevant detail or skipped by, as though it were material for beginners only, because no matter what our standard of play we cannot ignore such a fundamental factor. In fact I would recommend anyone to take some lessons in the Alexander technique, which is a method for improving the way we use our bodies. Under the guidance of an expert teacher we discover how to change the habits which hamper our freedom. I myself have found this to be of invaluable assistance.

RELEASING THE HIP AND KNEE JOINTS

Having removed unnecessary tension from our posture we are ready to assume the stance itself. The sole function of the stance is to prepare the way for free movement, so we will be looking at it in terms of how well it promotes this aim.

Freedom of movement is fostered by the presence of two seemingly contradictory characteristics in the stance — stability and mobility. In the lower half of the body we need a steady, well-balanced base capable of securely carrying the body, and in the upper half we need to be relaxed and mobile. You could compare the stance to a tree with its roots firmly in the ground and its upper limbs free and flexible.

Now let us see how we can maximise stability and mobility in our stance. We will begin by learning to fold the body using the hip and knee joints as hinges. These two natural hingeing points are vitally important since they allow us to assume a perfectly balanced stance with the minimum of tension.

Bending at the knees is not likely to give us too much trouble. However releasing your hip joint may be unfamiliar because the vast majority of us habitually bend over by curving or collapsing the back instead of using the joints. In fact many people are unsure as to the exact location of the hip joint, mistakenly thinking it is somewhere in the waist area. It is however much lower down — a ball and socket joint at the top of each leg, where the legs join on to the torso. You can find it by using your fingertips to follow the line of the groin in a curve around to the side, about the line taken by the leg of your underpants.

In order to gain some feeling for the use of the hip joint I would like you to try the following 'flying' exercise. With knees well flexed, first tilt your pelvis forward and lean back slightly. Then sweep your arms back like wings and swing the buttocks back and up, allowing the torso to tilt forward onto the legs (*pic 7*). I must stress that there is no holding back of the head. It must be relinquished so that the weight of the body can be taken on the legs, which will feel well used particularly in the thigh area. Do this exercise quickly several times, swinging vigorously from the hip hinge so that you develop a feeling for the release of this pivotal point of the body. My young nephew gave me the idea for this exercise, running

7 The 'flying' exercise.

around the garden pretending to be an aeroplane in this very position.

It may take some time to learn to release the hip hinge because it has in many cases become rusty through under-use. One way to test that we have actually released the joint instead of bending the back is to feel for the little channel in the lumbar area of our lower back. If we have collapsed the back it will feel like a rocky road with the vertebrae poking out, whereas if the hip joint has been released correctly there will be a smooth channel.

We are now ready to learn a coordinated release of the hip and knee joints in order to form a golf stance. To begin, check your posture, making sure that your knees are slightly flexed and your weight is evenly distributed. Then allow your head to nod forward as you bend your knees and at the same time release your hip joint. This allows the buttocks to glide backwards and the torso to fold forward (pic 8). The feeling is one of going back and down, giving over the weight of the torso to the legs. The release of the joints should not be forced, it is simply a matter of allowing the body to fold at its natural hingeing points. To help you do this try breathing out audibly as you fold your body down like a concertina, trusting your legs to carry its weight. The legs can best do this if the knees bend over the feet. The knock-kneed stance that has been recommended in many golfing manuals gives a wobbly feeling in the legs and collapses the arches of the feet, hardly a recipe for stability.

How do we know if we have assumed our stance correctly? For example you might ask 'Have I over- or under-used the hip and knee joints?' Here are some suggestions for testing your stance. If you have assumed it with a free relinquishing of the hip and knee joints there is a look of angularity at the groin. In a good stance I find that my trousers are highly creased in this area. With this goes a taut feeling in the thighs, since the weight of the body is being well carried by these strong muscles. You can also reach around and check that you have a smooth channel in the lumbar region. In addition you will have a light springy feeling in the feet since weight is distributed evenly over each foot (from heel to toe) and between both feet. From this position you will feel ready to pounce.

If the movement has been dominated by a release of the hip

8 A perfect Hip and Knee stance.
9 Too much hip release and too little knee bend leads to a feeling of totteriness. Compare this stance to 8 and you will see the subtle differences particularly in the knee area and the distance the hands hang from the body.

joint *(pic 9)*, your legs will feel tight but not able to carry you and weight will be centralised on your toes — you will feel ready to totter rather than pounce. If on the other hand the stance has been dominated by the knee bend with insufficient release at the hip joint *(pic 10)*, there will be little angularity, you will have a sluggish 'dead leg' feeling, weight will be centralised on your heels and you will feel some strain around the knees.

Of all the indicators to look for the feet are perhaps the most important. We need to learn to use them as sense organs since they acutely register the body's state of balance. I have to admit when I first started playing golf it never occurred to me to think of my feet, but the further I go the more I realise the vital role they play. As evidence of this point you will notice that good

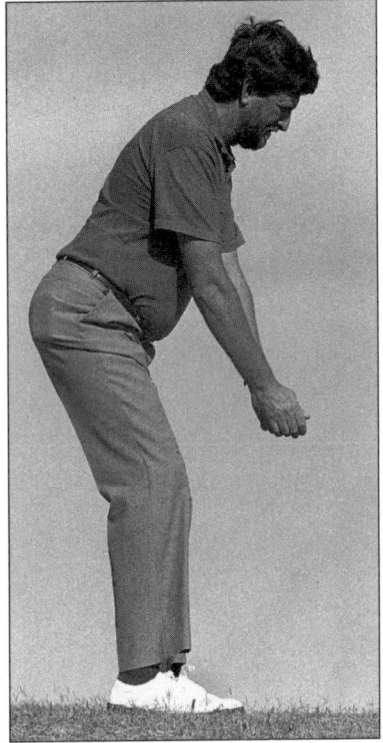

10 Without sufficient hip release the torso is practically upright.
11 The 'tail out' stance. Notice the exaggerated curve of the lower back, just above the belt, in comparison to 8.

players are continually moving their feet as they assume a stance in order to minutely adjust the distribution of their weight.

At this point I must mention one problem many people have in the stance, and that is the development of too great a lumbar curve — by which I mean there is a big sway in the lower back and the appearance of the tail being poked out *(pic 11)*. This has its origin in our standing posture. If we habitually stand in the 'tail out' position we automatically carry this through into our stance. The tension thus created in the lower back will then block the free use of this powerful part of the body in the swing. When people have this problem I get them to go back to their posture and work on re-aligning their pelvis so that the lower back has a less pronounced curve and the stomach muscles are in better tone.

When looking at the width of the stance we again need to combine the qualities of stability and mobility. It has to be wide enough to ensure stability but not so wide as to destroy freedom of movement or mobility. As a general principle you should have your feet spread to about the width of your shoulders. However, rules are of no consequence in this game. You need to learn to perceive in your own body the width of stance that enhances both stability and freedom of

12 The popular but deadly 'hunched stoop' stance.

movement. I have noticed when teaching that pupils who make poor use of their hip and knee joints attempt to compensate for the lack of stability inherent in their stance by widening it excessively. Then as their use of the joints improves, their feeling of security is enhanced, and they are able to narrow the stance considerably.

In contrast to my method of assuming a stance, the vast majority of golfers initiate the movement by simply bending their back and make little use of their hip and knee joints. This results in the body taking on a somewhat hunched appearance — in fact I call this stance the 'hunched stoop' *(pic 12)*. In my experience this approach has serious drawbacks if we aim to create a swing that embodies the qualities of balance, relaxation and rhythm. So let us now look at the advantages of the hip and knee release and compare it to the rather hunched way in which most golfers assume their stance.

The advantages of the hip and knee stance

Relaxation

The stance I recommend allows the torso to remain relaxed. This is because in actively using the joints rather than the muscles of the back to initiate movement, we free the torso from direct muscular activity and therefore from tension. A relaxed torso is essential since it needs to be free from tension in order to work as the axle of the swing. A free axle facilitates a flow of movement between the two sets of powerful muscles in the body — the ones around the shoulders, and the large muscles that join onto the pelvis.

By contrast a bending of the back to initiate the stance creates tension in the torso and robs the swing of its free axle. It is therefore impossible for the body's two sets of strong muscles to act in a coordinated way. So not only has relaxation been lost but also the possibility of rhythm and power.

Balance and stability

The stance I recommend aids balance and stability in two ways. Firstly, in using our hip and knee joints to fold the body down, we lower the whole body and thus lower our centre of gravity (a point about which our weight is centred, located near our belly button). This increases our stability because the lower our centre of gravity, the greater the force required to destabilise us. Thus racing cars are built lower to the ground than furniture vans! However, if we fail to lower the body using the joints and instead initiate the stance high in the body with a bend of the back, our centre of gravity remains high. We then have insufficient stability to make a free uninhibited swing.

Secondly, when we release the hip and knee joints our

strong leg muscles are actively used to carry the weight of the body, thus providing the swing with a stable base of support. This position gives us a feeling of power and strength in the legs and therefore a sense of being ready to pounce. In the hunched stoop, however, the strength of the leg muscles is not effectively used to carry the body. In this position our legs feel weak and spindly, and the lack of stability in the lower limbs once again leads to a rather defensive swing.

Space

By using the hip and knee joints to fold the body we create space in which the arms are able to hang and swing freely *(pic 13a)*. In the hunched stoop, on the other hand, the back is curved over and one could describe the body as having moved in on itself. As a result, little space is created, leading to a rather cramped swing *(pic 13b)*. This loss of space is often compensated for by pushing the arms away from the body, thus creating additional tension in the arms and shoulders *(pic 13c)*.

By now I hope the importance of an effective use of the hip and knee joints is clear to you. Far from being an arbitrary decision of mine, this stance is the logical result of examining the laws which govern movement. If we are off balance, tense, and have no room to work in, we simply cannot move freely, and no amount of tips or trickery will change that. It is only by using the joints that we gain the freedom to move. In fact it is the first thing I look for when teaching because I know all too well that unless this essential building block is securely in place, the swing is on shaky ground.

The common link with other sports

The position I have been describing is not peculiar to a golf stance. In its broad principles we share it with many other sports. An ability to move quickly and easily requires a ready position which uses the joints effectively and therefore maximises the qualities of balance and relaxation. I am sure that

13a The relaxed space created by the Hip and Knee stance.

you will recognise the same basic position in many sports all the way from ten-pin bowling to weight lifting.

Practising the golf stance

In order to make this new stance truly effective it is essential that we become extremely familiar with the movement. For this to occur, as with our posture, we need to integrate it into the way we use our bodies in everyday situations. For example if we learn to always bend using the hip and knee joints we will give ourselves at least one hundred opportunities a day to practise our golf stance and at the same time transfer the

13b The loss of space and tension in the 'hunched stoop'.

muscular effort required for bending and lifting to the strong leg muscles. The fact that most adults use the back to bend over, thus placing great strain on the relatively weak back muscles, could in part account for the large number of people who suffer from problems in the lower back area.

I realise that it is difficult to break old habits but each time you bend I would like you to stop and give yourself a simple reminder — 'Release the hip and knee joints'. In this way you will be utilising every opportunity to practise your golf stance and at the same time reducing the possibility of unnecessary back strain. This approach to bending may seem contrived at first

13c Plenty of space but at the expense of considerable tension.

but let me assure you that it is a natural way to use the body, so natural in fact that it was precisely the method you used as a child any time you wanted to pick something up *(pic 14)*.

THE GRAVITATIONAL HANG OF THE ARMS

Once we know how to release our hip and knee joints and thus be actively supported on our legs, it is time to remove unnecessary tension from the hands, arms and shoulders, the parts of our anatomy that actually transmit the blow. To do this, allow your arms to hang freely in the space created by the angular folding of your body, with gravity determining where they fall *(pic 15)*. Imagine your arms are lengths of rope hanging

14 Children instinctively fold at the joints.

loosely from your shoulder sockets. In this position the arms and shoulders are doing no work, they are completely relaxed and therefore able to swing freely. By contrast if the arms are tensed in any way the muscles are already in use (holding tension) and thus have a reduced capacity to swing freely.

I would now like you to conduct a small experiment. Take up your stance again and allow your hands and arms to hang freely where they will, gorilla-style. Gently swing your arms to and fro, letting your shoulders go and allowing your body to respond naturally to the rhythm of the swing. The movement should feel relaxed, natural and relatively effortless. Next, repeat the experiment with your arms pushed away from their free

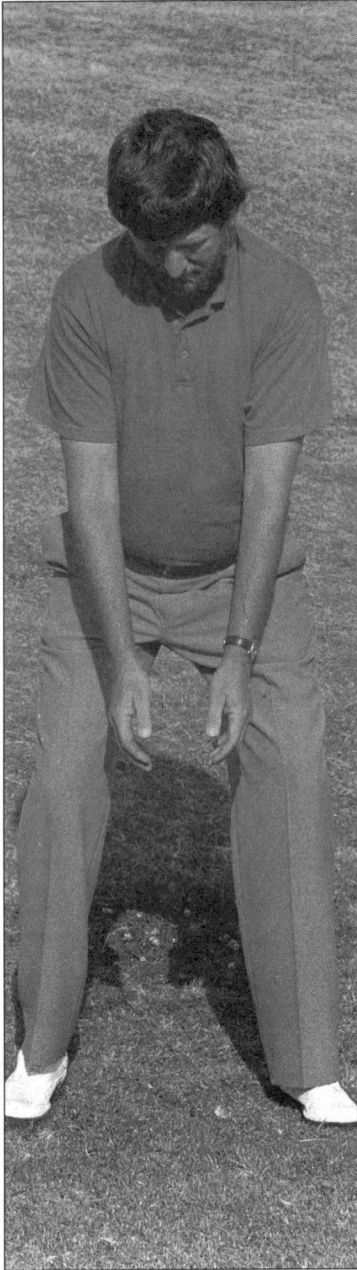

15 The gravitational hanging of the arms.

hanging point. You will find that the effortless rhythm of the previous swing has been replaced by a rather poky movement. This is because the muscle tension required to hold the arms in a pre-determined position has distorted the natural flow of the swing.

From this simple experiment you will have seen how important it is for the arms to establish a free hanging point from which they are able to move effortlessly in an uncontrived way. This kind of movement forms the basis of an easeful and powerful swing which is repeatable on every occasion. I will now show you how to introduce the club to your stance while at the same time retaining this highly desirable characteristic — the free gravitational hang of the arms.

The left arm, hand and shoulder

(Note that all references to left and right hands, arms and so on presuppose a right-handed player.)

As we have just seen, what we are looking for is not so much a position for the left arm but a way in which it can hang effortlessly from the shoulder. As far as the hand is concerned, what we want is not a 'grip' as such but a way of balancing the club using the minimum tension possible. In my view the role of the hands in a golf swing is to balance the club and to register fine differences of feeling as we strike the ball. If we are strangling the club with tension there is little likelihood of developing the subtle sensitivity of touch that is so essential, particularly in the delicate shots close to the green.

I would like you to take up your stance in the way I have suggested and allow your left arm to relax. Imagine it hanging loosely like a length of rope from the shoulder, and in the same way imagine your hand falling freely from the wrist joint. Leave your hand and arm hanging passively and gently cup the fingers slightly in order to create a channel for the club *(pic 16)*. Now take the club in your right hand and place it in this specially prepared channel without in any way moving, tensing or twisting the left hand, arm or wrist. The fingers are then delicately folded about the club with only sufficient finger pressure necessary to support the club. I must stress that the left hand is not actively used to grab the club, it merely receives it *(pic 17)*. In this way we have introduced the club while retaining the relaxed characteristics of the left arm, wrist and hand. In addition we are holding the club with the minimum amount of effort, because it is balanced between the index finger and the fleshy pad of the hand. This way of introducing the club also establishes a straight line from the point of the left shoulder to the end of the clubshaft. The only thing that remains to be done is to correctly adjust the angle of the clubface. You can check this by lifting the club off the ground to shoulder height and making sure that the bottom edge of the club is straight up and down, at 90° to the ground *(pic 18)*.

At this point I cannot emphasise enough that, rather than passively receiving the club, it is all too easy to unconsciously

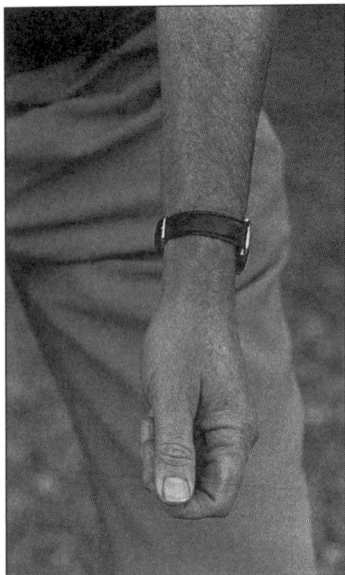

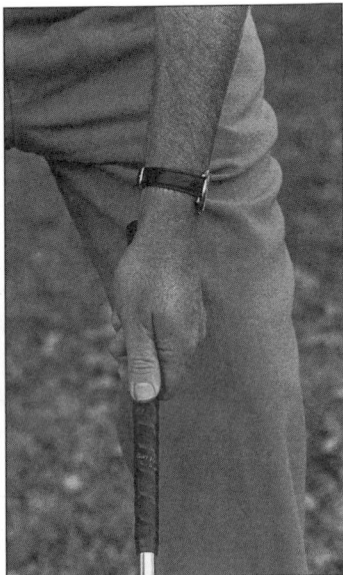

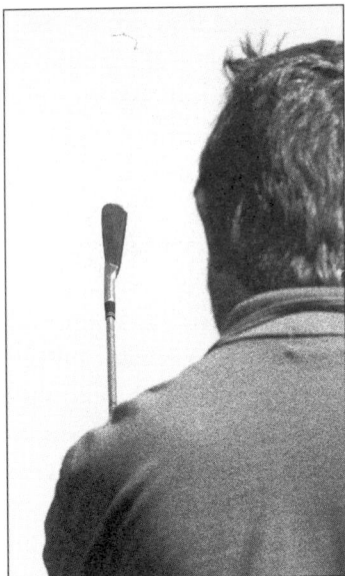

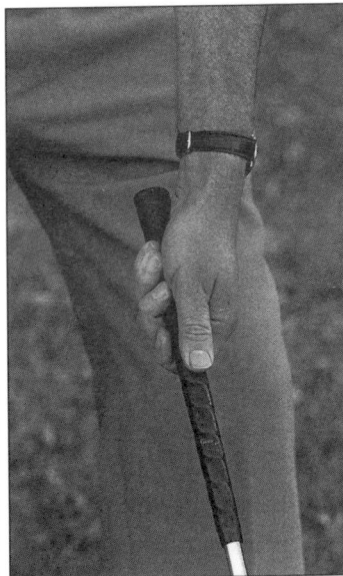

16 The left hand is now ready to receive the club.   **17** The club now housed in its special channel.
18 The leading edge of the club needs to be straight up and down.
19 Compare this to 17. Here a twisting of the wrist means the top of the grip is no longer cushioned by the fleshy pad of the hand.

make a grab for it with the left hand (in fact most people tend to do this). So let us examine the far-reaching effects of even a small divergence from the totally relaxed position described above. Firstly, the slightest grasping for the club will twist the hand and so prevent us from using its fleshy pad to balance the club *(pic 19)*. We will then inevitably have to use finger pressure to compensate for the loss of the stabilising and cushioning effect of the fleshy pad. This introduces unnecessary tension into the grip, thus reducing the free use of the wrist joint and preventing us from feeling the clubhead with sufficient sensitivity.

Secondly, any time we make a grab for the club we inevitably turn the wrist slightly and this tenses the muscles of the forearm, robbing us of both power and feeling. Try it out for yourself and observe how even a small turn of the wrist twists and tenses these muscles. Finally, any grasping for the club necessarily moves the left hand away from its free hanging point and across to meet the club. As we will see later in detail, the maintenance of this free hanging point, which establishes a straight line from the point of the left shoulder to the end of the club, is of vital importance to the coordinated use of the body.

Before we leave the subject of the left arm I must point out that it is a common error to think it is hanging freely when it is not. By this I mean that we tend to put our arm where we think it 'should' be rather than taking the trouble to let it fall and rediscover its free-hanging point every time. For example, I find that any time I presume that the left arm is all right because I know roughly where it hangs, it ends up further and further away from its free-hanging position, and I am astonished, when I fully let the arm go, to discover the amount of error that has crept in unconsciously. So we can never rely on memory to produce a relaxed position, rather we have to give our full attention to the task of allowing tension to drop away and so rediscover a free-hanging point afresh on each occasion.

The right hand, arm and shoulder

The right hand is placed lower down the clubshaft than the left, so we need to find a way of bringing it across to the club without either creating tension in the right hand, arm or shoulder, or shortening the left arm. I have found that the only way to do this is to re-align the body slightly, so that the right arm and hand fall at a lower point than the left. The right arm is then swung across like a pendulum to meet the club. In this way we are able to introduce the right hand, arm and shoulder without tension creeping in.

The re-alignment of the body is initiated by a small see-saw-like tilting of the collar-bone . This causes the left shoulder to come up slightly and the right down *(pic 20)*. To avoid any lurching of the body sideways it is helpful to place a finger in the little triangular hollow in the centre of the collar-bone, and to imagine that as the apex of a see-saw. The apex needs to stay where it is without moving from side to side as the tilt of the collar-bone takes place.

Practise this movement a number of times until you get a clear feeling of the response of the shoulders to the tilt of the collar-bone. Then introduce a club into your freely hanging left hand and re-align the shoulders in this way. Since this causes the whole left arm to move up a fraction, you need to leave about an inch and a half of shaft protruding above the level of the left hand, and to loosen your fingers so that they can slide up the shaft as the re-alignment takes place *(pic 21)*.

Now let your right arm hang like a length of rope with the hand falling freely from the wrist joint. Without twisting or turning the shoulder, arm, wrist or hand in any way swing your arm across from the shoulder like a pendulum to meet the club. I must stress that your head stays where it is and the right arm swings past it on its way across to meet the left *(pic 22)*. If you have made the necessary degree of re-alignment, the three large fingers of the right hand are able to join the club just

20 Before and after tilting the collar-bone. Here I
have used a club to highlight the movement.
21 Leave about an inch and a half of shaft
protruding above the left hand before re-aligning
the body.

22 The pendulum-like right arm swings across to meet the club. Note that the head does not move.

below the index finger of the left hand *(pic 23)*. However if you have made too small a tilt only one or two fingers will be able to join directly onto the club; too large a movement will result in all four fingers on the club. It is a matter of experimenting, adjusting the degree of re-alignment until you are able to swing the passive right arm across and gain a perfect tension-free fit.

Let us now look at the placement of the right hand in more detail. As with the left hand, we are not looking for a set way of gripping the club, but are seeking to find a relaxed and secure position that will not create tension in the muscles of the right hand, arm or shoulder. As we have seen, the three large fingers fit snugly up against the index finger of the left hand. The little finger is allowed to find a comfortable position on top of the index finger of the left hand. Its exact position is not important, in fact no special attempt should be made to bed the little finger

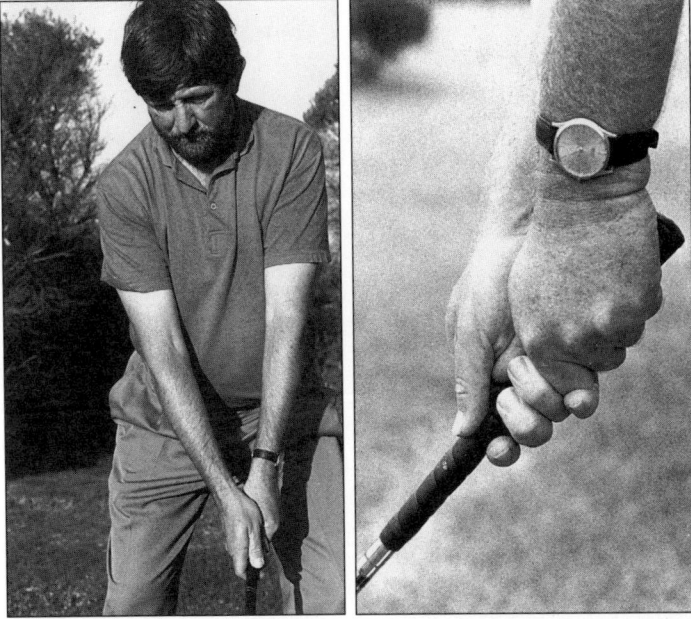

23 The ideal degree of re-alignment allows the two hands to fit perfectly together, with no gaps or overlaps.

in between the index and middle finger of the left hand, as that will spread our hand too widely over the grip *(pic 24)*.

What is important is the relationship between the right thumb and index finger. The crook of the index finger forms a balancing point for the club, which is held in place by a slight downward pressure of the right thumb. The latter fits snugly up against the index finger. This is the only way to secure the club without using unnecessary tension. If we move the thumb away from the index finger, as many people do, it creates a massive hole in which the club wobbles uncontrollably. This often happens when the wrist is twisted slightly and the hand is attached under the shaft *(pic 25)*. Any turning of the wrist whatsoever inevitably tenses the muscles of the forearm and will inhibit a free swing of the arms. Experiment with it yourself and see the effects of even a small amount of distortion in these muscles.

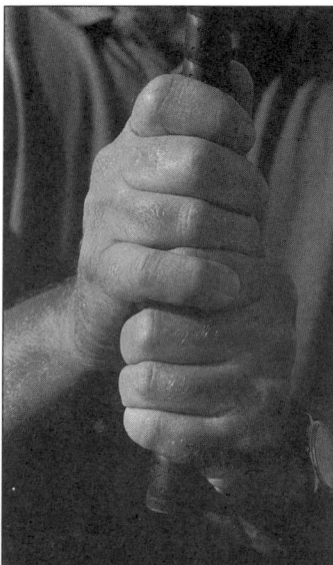

Top 24a Too much of an attempt to accommodate the little finger can cause the powerful ring finger to lose contact with the grip.   **24b** A snug fit of both hands on the club.
Bottom 25a and **b** In these two photos compare the relationship between the index finger and the thumb on the right hand. In 25a there is a gap for the club to move uncontrollably in, whereas in 25b we have a close supportive relationship which provides firmness and stability without tension.

As with the left hand, we are definitely not gripping the club but balancing it, using the minimum finger pressure possible. Excessive pressure tightens up the hands, arms and shoulders so the arms are not loose enough to swing freely. As we saw earlier, our aim is to establish an absolutely free swing of the arms, and this can only happen when we learn to balance the club rather than grip or grasp it.

You may find that the stance I recommend feels a little awkward at first. This is in part due to the fact that a relaxed way of doing things often cuts across our habitual patterns and therefore can feel strange and uncomfortable. It is our habitual ways that we find comfortable, even if they create tension. We may feel comfortable slouching in an armchair, for example, yet our spine is twisted and our back collapsed. So it is dangerous to equate comfort with relaxation, because in feeling comfortable we are often being drawn back into our old familiar ways of doing things.

The other reason why this stance may feel awkward and even slightly insecure is that it favours the left side of the body. By this I mean the left arm is our long or strong arm. In addition, since our head is behind the ball, we are looking at it more with our left eye — in other words we are looking at the back of the ball. Favouring the left side cuts against our instinct (if we are right-handed) to control the situation by having our stronger right side in the dominant position. There are, however, severe drawbacks when we give in to our right-handedness, as we often do unconsciously. Firstly the left hand tends to involuntarily move across to the right (instead of vice versa as I recommend), then the whole right side of the body moves over and across as we go to grasp the club. This is an active grab for the club, not the passive tension-free fit which I suggest. Giving in to our right-handedness in this way also results in a bent left arm, our head over the ball, with the right eye looking down on top of the ball in severe cases, and a right arm that is stretched over to meet the club *(pic 26)*.

26a and **b** In 26a the right hand and arm have taken over, whereas in 26b the left side of the body has assumed the dominant position. Note the line from the point of the left shoulder to the end of the stick in 26b, and the carriage of the head behind the ball.

In my experience, the unconscious need to dominate with the right side is a significant problem for many golfers. Our right side represents security or control and we tend to gravitate to it, since it is the side on which we feel safer. Left-handed golfers have the same problems in reverse. Let us now look at the advantages of my approach to the stance and see why it is important to place our trust in the relatively weaker left side of our body.

The advantages of this approach to the hands, arms and shoulders

Shoulder alignment

Tilting the collar-bone in the way I recommend and swinging

27 The ideal alignment of the body. Here the target is the first bush to the right of the gap.

the right arm across to meet the left result quite naturally in a perfect alignment of the shoulders. By this I mean that they are pointing in the same direction as the hips and feet, slightly to the left of target *(pic 27)*.

However, if we skimp on preparation and give in to right-handedness, we move our right arm, shoulder and our head over and across so that we can attach our right hand to the club. This action inevitably results in the shoulders pointing too far to the left of the target. This malalignment has in part caused the slice to become golf's most common result!

Power

From the position I recommend the left arm will stay basically straight and will naturally assume the dominant role in the backswing, with the right arm bending and remaining relatively close to the body. As we will see in detail in the next chapter, this brings the right arm into what I call the 'karate chop' position — that is a position close to the body from which it is able to straighten quickly in the latter stages of the downswing, hence providing explosive power on impact. By contrast, if we make a grab for the club with the right hand, the right arm tenses and straightens and it is then difficult for it to bend in the desired way. In traditional terms this has been described as a 'flying right elbow'. It is then impossible to achieve the vital karate chop position on the way down, and the explosive power generated by a release of the right elbow is replaced by a rather weak flicking action.

Coordination

The method I have suggested creates a straight line from the point of the left shoulder to the end of the club. This is important since it ensures that the hands, arms and shoulders swing together in a coordinated way on the backswing, and thus increases the potential for a more powerful swing. In this way what has been described as the 'one piece takeaway', in which the hands, arms and shoulders move together at the start of the swing, will occur quite naturally *(see pic 26b)*. However if we move the left hand across to meet the club at a mid point in the stance, the hands end up behind the ball and the vital line from shoulder to clubhead is broken. This makes it impossible for the swing to commence with a coordinated movement in the arms and shoulders. Instead the hands take a dominant role in the swing and do the majority of the work, resulting in the club being picked up and hence a swing that could only be described as a wristy chopping action.

Extending the arc of the swing

This method fully extends the arc of the swing. If we think of the line from the left shoulder to the clubhead as the radius of the swing then it follows that the longer we are able to make our radius, the wider will be the sweep or arc of the swing. The only way to fully extend the radius is to ensure a straight alignment of the left arm and clubshaft.

This brings me to the well-known advice 'Take the clubhead back low to the ground'. If you take up your stance in the way I suggest you will have a fully extended radius, and as a result your backswing arc will automatically widen. In this situation the clubhead will of its own accord stay close to the ground in the early part of the swing.

If we give in to our right-handedness, we destroy the alignment of the left arm and clubshaft. Thus we shorten the radius of the swing and reduce the width of the arc (see pic 26a).

Sensitivity of feeling

The final advantage of introducing the club into your stance in this way is that it is relaxing, and thus allows you to feel the clubhead more acutely. The greater the degree of relaxation in the hands and arms the greater will be your awareness of the clubhead. If we think of the club as a tool, say a chisel or a needle, then in order to use it with craftsman-like skill we need to know exactly what it is doing. To know what it is doing we need to be aware of it, and relaxation is the vital quality which increases our awareness and allows us to fashion our shot with delicacy and precision.

By contrast, traditional methods dictate a set way of gripping the club. The word 'grip' itself has unfortunate connotations since it implies a tight grasping of the club, which in my view is incompatible with the need to be sensitively aware of the clubhead. However my principal objection to the traditional approach is that it ignores the fact that we all have hands of differing shapes and sizes, so what might be appropriate for one person will not be relaxed for another. Not only does this deny individuality, but also trying to imitate a recommended pattern ('trying to get it right') inevitably creates tension. So I have not told you what is a 'correct grip', but rather shown you how to establish for yourself a relaxed position of the hands which will by its very nature maximise the free use of the hands, arms and shoulders.

Rediscovering the stance afresh

The hip and knee release and the relaxed introduction of the club are in themselves very simple. However in order to perform them without tension filtering in we need to bring our full attention to what we are doing each time we assume our stance. The major problem is that our mind tends to wander. We find it easy to presume that things can be left to take care of themselves, in other words, we want to go to sleep and switch into an automatic mode. When this occurs tension-bearing habits start to creep in unnoticed. For example I am constantly reminded, both in my own game and when teaching, how easy it is to unconsciously give in to our right-handedness and move the left arm across to meet the right hand, thus destroying the alignment of the left arm. The only way to prevent unconscious habits such as this from taking over is to become more fully aware of our tendencies in this area by keenly observing and feeling what we are actually doing. The same degree of awareness is necessary with our posture and the release of the hip and knee joints.

So I cannot emphasize enough that the stance can only be performed with the degree of accuracy required when you give your full attention to the task. We are all constantly tempted to drift into a semi-conscious state and let things happen by themselves, but it is essential to go into our feelings and rediscover the stance freshly each time we make it. In short, assuming a relaxed and balanced stance is a disciplined process requiring us to give our full awareness from moment to moment. By taking the trouble to do this we will be richly rewarded, since it paves the way for the emergence of a truly free and expressive swing.

3

The

Swing

THE DETAILED PREPARATION I have described so far has been designed to remove unnecessary tension and improve balance, and thus create the best possible conditions for the emergence of your individual swing. The wrist joints are now free to hinge, the arms are able to swing from the shoulders, the torso is able to work as the channel or axle of the swing, the powerful pelvic muscles are ready and willing to lend their strength, and last but not least we are actively supported on our legs and have a secure footing from which to move. So in a highly disciplined way we have set the body up to move freely.

In order to fully utilise these favourable conditions we now need to turn our attention to rhythm — the third vital quality for the growth of your swing. As I said earlier, rhythm brings to our swing the power of coordinated movement, a predictable beat and the pleasure of freedom and spontaneity. But what exactly is rhythm? The word itself comes from the Greek 'rhythmos' meaning 'to flow'. I often describe rhythm as a harmonising force which links movement together so that the body is able to work as a flowing whole, rather than as a collection of parts. Rhythm is not something that we can consciously control, it is an instinctive beat to which we need to surrender. As you increasingly learn to move to the beat of your own internal clock your swing will gain a feeling of ease, and the power generated will take you by surprise. You will have noticed, for example, when watching the professionals play how easy they make it look, and may have experienced in your own game that the best shots seem to come from an essentially easy and simple swing. It is as though your natural rhythmic swing revealed itself spontaneously in that moment. My task is to show you how to make this extremely pleasurable experience a more regular occurrence.

Since rhythm is a bodily pulse which cannot be consciously controlled, how can we develop a rhythmic swing? In my view we can only let go and abandon ourselves to a rhythmic flow of movement when we feel truly confident in our body's ability to do the job for us. So our first task will be to gain confidence in the natural functioning of our body. In order to do this we will be working, principally through slow-motion exercises, on increasing our awareness of the body — feeling every movement intimately and experiencing the subtle interrelationship between various parts of the body in a coordinated golf swing. In this way we will build up faith in our body's ability to swing the club for us.

Secondly, having discovered what the movement feels like, we will be learning to relinquish all thought of conscious control of the swing, allowing the natural rhythm of the body to flow free and unimpeded. In a sense the swing has to swing you. As a pupil of mine aptly put it, 'You have to swing with an empty mind' rather than self-consciously constructing the movement. In the same way concert pianists do not work on technique during a performance, they need to have done that well in advance so that they are free to give themselves fully to a sensitive interpretation of the music.

As you will have gathered, my method of teaching a golf swing is completely at variance with the traditional view of the situation. The latter approach attempts to construct a 'perfect' swing by dictating a complicated set of instructions which we are required to copy. Most of you will be familiar with these instructions such as 'Keep your head down, left arm straight, hit against a firm left side, extend the arc of the swing through the ball,' etcetera. The swing thus becomes a series of fragmented sections like the pieces of a jig-saw puzzle, and we become preoccupied with getting it right — putting all the pieces together in their correct order. In this situation we inevitably become stiff and mechanical since movement loses its natural spontaneity and becomes something to be controlled rather than enjoyed. Mechanical movement, as well as being unsatisfying inwardly, is in my experience totally ineffective since the movements of a golf swing are too complex and occur far too quickly for the conscious mind to fully comprehend, let alone control. It would be like trying to run up a flight of stairs while at the same time self-consciously working out each part of the movement. For this reason I feel that it is impossible to learn to play golf by 'trying to do it properly'.

I am not denying that the conscious mind has a role to play. However, rather than imposing on the body a preconceived pattern to be copied, the mind's role is to understand the natural functioning of the body and understand it so well that we can relinquish conscious control and trust the body to do its job unimpeded. I must emphasise that real trust is always based on understanding, one can only truly relinquish to something when one understands it. So we need to begin by gaining an acute awareness of our body in movement.

The first thing I want to make you aware of is what it feels like to have your body moving as a coordinated whole with your hands, arms, shoulders, hips, legs and feet moving together. Since most people mistakenly believe that a golf swing is an affair principally of the hands, arms and shoulders, we must pay particular attention to fully integrating the powerful muscles of the lower half of the body (hips and legs) into the movement.

I would like you to take up your stance without a club, allowing your arms to hang gorilla-style from the shoulders. Imagine your torso as a barrel which is able to rotate. Now allow your barrel to start turning and as it rotates back and forth let your arms swing in perfect time to it and feel your feet dance as weight shifts from one foot to another. Simply abandon yourself to the free and spontaneous nature of this movement with no holding back. Thus the arms are swinging freely, they are not pushed back and forth. The same applies to the hips, they are not forced to turn but allowed to flow with the upper body. In this way the whole body moves as one. Nothing is being made to happen, limbs are not mechanically positioned: rather, the whole organism is operating freely.

Now let us focus our entire attention on the movement of our 'barrel' because in my experience most people lack sufficient awareness of this area of the body. Yet the efficient use of the torso is vitally important for two reasons. Firstly it houses the body's strongest muscles, so one might describe the barrel as the power source or engine of the swing. In the same way a discus thrower really winds up and releases his throw from this part of the body. Secondly, it houses our centre of gravity, the point (near our belly button) about which the weight of our body is concentrated. As you will see, when we move from our barrel or centre we maintain perfect poise, and conversely if we leave our centre behind or out of the movement we lose our balance. Anyone who does tai chi or a martial art will be familiar with this important role of the centre.

So, take up your stance without a club. Put your right hand just below your belly button and your left hand across your collar-bone with the thumb on the left side and your fingers on the right side. Slowly turn your barrel round, so that your whole torso moves as one piece. Feel your right leg acting as a pillar securing the movement as your back turns to face the target. To start down, return to your stance position with weight equally carried on both feet and then continue rotating your whole axle until your belly faces the target *(pic 28)*. I have found it useful to practise this exercise for a few minutes a day in order to build up my awareness of this essential core of the swing.

28 The 'barrel' exercise.

29 The starting position for the slow-motion exercise. You can imagine you are gently holding a ball.

The Half Swing

We are now ready to re-integrate the arms and begin work on a slow-motion golf swing without a club. I would like you to move sensuously and very slowly indeed in this exercise, giving your entire attention to feeling, because the aim is to help you experience the workings of your own body. It is as though we are going inside and concentrating entirely on feelings. It is extremely helpful to practise without shoes in order to feel more acutely where the weight falls on the soles of your feet.

Take up your stance without a club, and focus on your sense of balance. Feel the springiness in your feet and the strength in your powerful thigh muscles. Allow your arms to hang gorilla-

30 Note the secure balancing of the body on the legs, and the relaxation in the arms.

style, and feel all tension fall away as they hang passively *(pic 29)*. Then, leaving your eyes looking at an imaginary ball, picture your barrel turning relaxedly as you slowly release it and allow your arms to swing or float back, moving slowly in response to the turn of the barrel. You will feel your weight moving onto the heel of your right foot and the ball of your left foot. You will feel your thigh muscles working overtime, actively supporting the body. Continue the movement until your arms are about shoulder high, then hold the position for a second and once again feel the strength in your legs and the distribution of weight on your feet *(pic 30)*. On the way down allow the barrel to lead slowly once again, with the arms moving passively in response. See how this immediately shifts

31 Here we move back to the stance position in the legs, with the arms lagging behind slightly.

weight — firstly equalising it so that it is carried on both feet *(pic 31)*, and then as the barrel turns past an imaginary ball and towards the target, weight moves onto the outer edge of the left foot, especially the heel, and the toe of the right foot. The arms merely react to the flow of the barrel and float slowly down and through, ending up shoulder-high.

It is very important to let the head go, allowing it to come up naturally as the swing flows through to its finish *(pic 32)*. Any attempt to keep the head down will block the forward momentum of the swing. You might like to experiment with exaggeratedly keeping your head down and see how it strangles the movement. Then on the next swing let it go and

32 A balanced finish to the swing, with the belly facing the target.

experience how you can release into an easeful follow-through. To a lesser extent the same is true of the backswing, because if the head is kept rigidly still it is impossible to turn our axle. Again try it for yourself and see how a head that stubbornly refuses to yield wrecks the swing. What we need is a slight rotation of the head to facilitate the turn of the axle. The eyes move in their sockets and look relaxedly at the ball. From this position it is almost as though we could take a bite out of the juicy flesh of our upper arm, whereas if the head is left behind there is nothing to get our teeth into *(pic 33)*.

It may feel rather weird at first, but I would now like you to repeat this slow-motion swing with your eyes closed, giving

33 A slight rotation of the head which allows the axle and in particular the shoulders to turn fully.

your full attention to your sense of balance. Removing vision in this way takes us more into sensing or feeling, so you will experience even more dramatically the relationship between the use of the centre and the flow of weight, and will appreciate more acutely the vital role your hips, legs and feet play in a golf swing. Try placing your right hand on your stomach just below the belly-button as you do this exercise — it will give you a strong feeling of contact with this important part of the body.

Next, with your eyes still closed, feel the effect on your balance when you hold the centre out of this movement by allowing your arms to swing as far as possible and at the same time stop any turn in the barrel. Hold it completely out of the movement and notice how quickly you feel off-balance and start to totter, as weight moves onto the outside edge of the right foot. You will feel insecure in your legs and feet, with no solid base of support. You will also find that you have no flexibility, and start to feel very tight in your arms and shoulders since they are burdened with all the work.

This last exercise is an exaggerated example of what happens in the average golfer's swing. Since the vast majority of people have difficulty in fully using the centre, their swing to some extent becomes a sway rather than a pivoting turn. In the absence of a freely turning 'barrel' on the backswing, the body has no choice but to sway, and hence the right knee moves across and weight shifts almost off the outside edge of the right foot (pic 34). It will take diligent practice to learn to fully use your centre, so I would like you to do the slow-motion exercise as frequently as possible. You can even practise in the shower, where you have the added advantage of seeing exactly what your body is doing, without your view being obscured by clothing. Your right knee can be used as a guide to how well you have turned on the backswing. If the barrel has pivoted freely it will stay in its original position with weight carried securely on the heel of the right foot. In the absence of an effective use of the centre, weight will move onto the outside edge of the right foot and the right knee sways laterally. However the right knee position is not an end in itself, merely a guide as to how well the barrel has turned, so there is no point in forcing it to do what you want. As you increasingly allow the centre to release, you will experience the ease and freedom that come when one learns to use this vital area of the body uninhibitedly.

Introducing a club

Our next task is to introduce the club to this half swing, once again slowing the action right down so that we can experience the movements of the body inch by inch. This time we are going to focus on our hands and arms and their role in the

34 A precariously balanced position in which the right leg can no longer support the body correctly.

swing. The hands merely support the weight of the club and do not directly manipulate the clubhead, since the ball needs to be hit with the larger muscles of the body and not with a flick of the wrists. The role of the arms is again not one of direct manipulation; rather, they react and swing freely in response to the turn of the centre which is the engine of the movement. So we will be working in this exercise on teaching the hands and arms their role in the swing.

I would like you to start by taking up your stance with a club. Feel the weight of your arms hanging from the shoulders. Lift the club off the ground slightly to feel its weight. The more gently you can hold the club the heavier it will seem. Now once again, leaving your eyes looking at an invisible ball, imagine your centre turning as you let your arms swing ever so slowly from the shoulders. Just do enough with your hands to prevent the club falling back towards the ground. Feel your whole body pivoting, with weight moving onto the ball of your left foot and heel of your right foot. Keep the turn going until the arms reach approximately shoulder high, then stop and once again focus on the weight of the club and feel yourself just holding it firmly enough to support its weight *(pic 35)*. The left arm will be fully extended but not dead straight, with the arm and clubshaft still in alignment. The right arm will be flexed, slightly bent at the elbow. The wrists have not been consciously broken as such but yield naturally in response to the flexing of the right elbow. I must reiterate that the hands are at all times merely balancing the club, and no attempt should be made to artificially place yourself in the position I have just described — it is only a guide to how you will be when your hands and arms have exercised their correct role.

Now start down slowly with your centre and get the feeling of leaving your arms behind momentarily. This causes the wrist break to increase slightly as the arms change direction and start to float down. The initiation of the downswing from the centre has caused weight to start moving onto the inside edge of your

35 Perfect balance at the top of the half swing.

right foot and the flat of your left foot. Hold the position and feel the strength in your legs and the poise of your body on your feet *(pic 36)*. This is what I describe as the 'karate chop' position because the right arm is bent and close to the side of the body, ready to straighten and provide the swing with explosive power. From this position it could be said that we are ready to pounce.

Now as your centre begins to turn towards the target, feel your right arm starting to straighten. Feel weight moving off the inside edge of your right foot and onto the outside edge and heel of your left foot. A combination of these two factors, a shift in weight and the karate chop or straightening of the right arm, enables you to release the full power of the swing

36 The 'karate-chop' position.

(pic 37). As the movement continues on past an imaginary ball, let your head go and feel the centre of your body turn increasingly towards the target. Feel more and more weight move onto the left foot, and allow the straightened right arm to take over from the left as the long arm of the swing *(pic 38)*.

I have found that many people can benefit from doing this exercise holding the club with their left hand alone, since this is the weaker side of the body for most right-handers and we therefore need to strengthen it. Placing your right hand on your belly-button area, pick the club up off the ground slightly so you are fully supporting its weight. Then allow your barrel to turn slowly and just keep the club supported. You will feel your wrist giving slightly, hingeing at the same time as

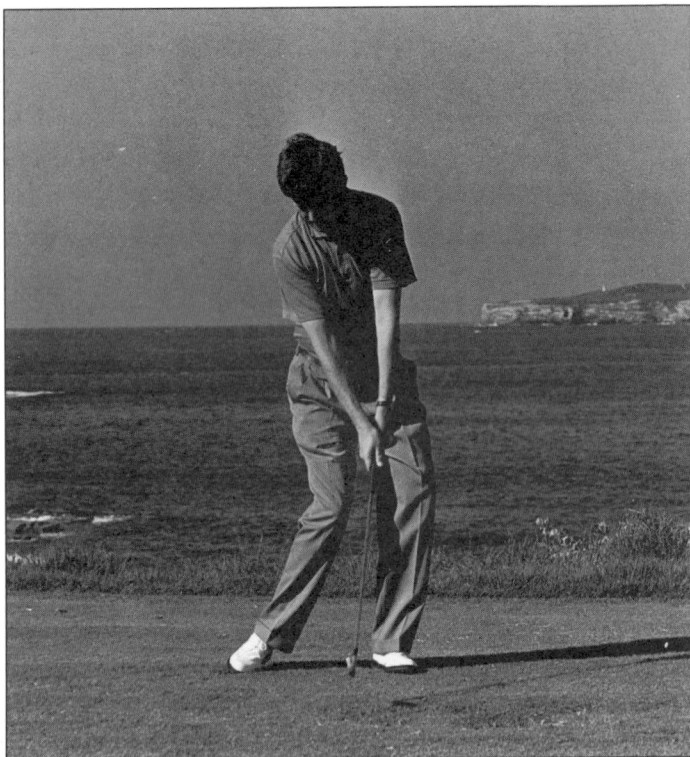

37 Even in slow-motion this impact position feels decisive and powerful.

supporting the club towards the top of your half swing. At this point there is a distinctive L shape between the shaft and the forearm *(pic 39)*. It is all too easy to start lifting the club up with the arm, whereas what we want is a turning of the trunk and a hingeing of the wrist. Any lifting of the club will result in the whole body lifting up out of the legs, thus compromising our balance. On the way down you might like to re-attach your right hand, and swing through as normal, since it becomes very hard work for the left arm alone! This exercise increases our awareness of the weaker side of the body and its important role in the formation of the backswing.

I must stress that it is no use doing all these exercises once or twice, nor merely doing them mechanically. You will have

38 The follow through of the half swing, a position we can hold for quite some time if we are well-balanced

to repeat them many times and give your complete attention to the feelings they produce in order to gain the sensitivity to your body that is vitally necessary. In fact if you stop practising in the mistaken belief that you have already got things worked out you will find that your sensitivity of feeling or awareness diminishes. This hard fact applies to us all, and so I need to continue my own work in this direction. As you will have realised, this is not a passive approach to learning the swing but rather an active discovery of the free use of your own body, and thus the discovery of your own swing.

Having gained a strong feeling of what coordinated movement feels like we are almost ready to work up the tempo of our half swing from slow-motion to normal speed. I must

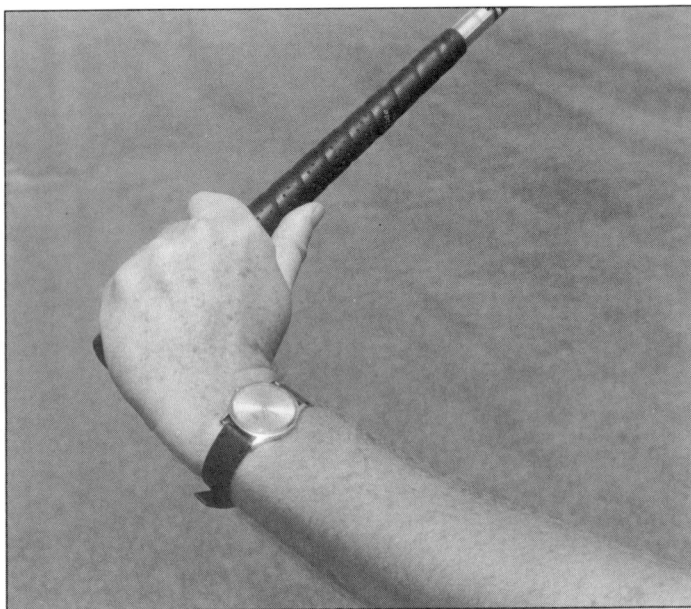

39 The L-shape in the left arm at the top of a half swing.

point out that this tempo will vary with each individual —
some people are naturally slow and languid while others have
a quick staccato beat. At normal speed (whatever that might
be) we have a fraction of a second to perform all the
movements that I have just described. In other words the swing
happens far too quickly to be controlled by the conscious
mind, and any attempt at this stage to analyse the movement
will inevitably paralyse us. So we need to learn to abandon all
thought of conscious control and instead tune our movements
in to the instinctive beat of our body. To help you to do this
we are going to use the rhythm of our breathing. By
concentrating on breathing we not only free our body by
diverting the conscious mind from analysis, but also give
ourselves a strong natural beat to follow, and we can focus our
attention on our centre

To ease ourselves in we will begin by tuning our slow-
motion swing to a rhythmic breathing pattern. As you slowly

swing back, breathe in deeply, imagining your barrel filling with air. Then store that air and as your centre turns towards the target, let it go and continue the swing on until it naturally runs out of forward momentum. It is as though we are taking in energy throughout the backswing and then releasing it through the ball. Some people may find it helpful to fill their mind with the word 'IN' to coincide with breathing in (then hold this energy), and the word 'OUT' for releasing the power of the swing. Practise this exercise repeatedly in slow-motion until a strong association builds up between your breathing and the parts of the swing. Breathing should not be forced — we are drawing it in and letting it go naturally. In this way our breathing mirrors the easeful quality we want in our swing.

It will also be helpful to spend some time practising the deep breathing by itself with your hands on your belly. Feel your abdomen expand as the air flows in and contract as it flows out. We need to learn to breathe right down into the centre in order to help activate it. Shallow breathing (which most of us are used to) leads to an uptight swing in which the energy of the body is stuck in the top of the chest.

We are now ready to apply this breathing pattern to a half swing at normal speed. Simply abandon yourself to the pattern of your breath as though you are 'breathing' your swing and allow movement to flow freely and uninhibitedly. The more you become engrossed in flowing with your breathing the more all thoughts of how to do it drift out of your mind, and in this way a swing emerges that is truly expressive of the natural rhythm of your body.

I would also like you to try varying the pattern of your breathing, and see the effect that this has on your body. Instead of breathing in on the backswing breathe out, hold, and then breathe in on impact. Your body will feel as though you are moving against its natural flow. Also try holding your breath for the entire swing. You will feel inhibited, unable to release, and maybe slightly anxious. Finally, re-tune your breathing to the rhythm of the body and enjoy the feeling of ease and freedom which this brings.

It will be clear to you from these experiments how important it is to actively use your breathing to help your swing flow freely. As you may know, breathing also has an important role in many other sports. One could not imagine a karate expert, for example, without the sudden and dramatic exhalation of breath and the accompanying roar which occur on contact with a pile of roof tiles! In tennis, Jimmy Connors breathed out quite aggressively each time he made contact with the ball. On a more mundane level, any time you lift something heavy you may find yourself unconsciously breathing in as you take up the strain, and letting your breath go as you release the tension.

I would now like you to continue with the rhythmic half swing but start to also imagine the result you require. Gain a strong image of the ball sitting on the ground and slowly and very carefully assume a balanced and relaxed stance. As before, take in energy as you breathe in on the backswing, then time your outbreath to coincide with contact with the invisible ball and 'see' it fly down the fairway.

We have now physically and psychologically prepared ourselves to hit a ball. All that remains to be done is to introduce a real ball. I find it is best to go into the stance routine — creating the appropriate body angle, hanging the arms and introducing the club — some little distance from the ball. Then edge up to the ball without changing these characteristics in any way. (If we make the ball our goal to start with we are apt to unconsciously push the arms away from the body in order to find the ball, thus destroying their gravitational hanging point.) Then it is a matter of tuning your swing to the rhythmic flow of your breathing and allowing yourself to hit the ball as you have just imagined.

You may feel that I have said too little about actually hitting the ball. However my principal point is that the shot itself needs to flow spontaneously out of the conditions of balance, relaxation and rhythm that we have so carefully created. Unfortunately the vast majority of us try to gain our ends by direct means, in other words, we focus on trying to hit the ball. Yet the harder we try the more tense and rigid our movements become, which has the effect of driving away any possibility of a favourable result. This has been well summed up by Fritz Perls' memorable phrase 'Trying fails!' The difficulty is that we have a life-long habit of trying behind us, and often do not know any other way of approaching a situation. In fact I can hear many of you saying 'If I don't try to do it, what do I do?' I feel the answer lies in learning to relinquish more and more control to the body. We need to *let* ourselves swing the club rather than make ourselves, trusting the body that we have so very well prepared to do the job for us. In the same way, when we speak or walk we just do it, we don't think about how. If we did we would be struck dumb or lame.

To help pupils over the problem of trying, I encourage them to miss the ball if necessary, to free themselves to 'fail' and to not care about the result. What is the difference if we miss the ball or play a bad shot? I have often noticed that just before a pupil hits their first really good shot they will make several abortive swings which from the teacher's point of view look good, but for some reason these swings miss-hit the ball. The pupil wants to know what is wrong with their swing. I have to encourage them in the belief that the swing is fine and they just have to wait until their first perfect shot is ready to come. Usually what happens is that the less they care about the result the more easily, to their surprise, it does come, and the swing with which they hit a perfect shot is indistinguishable from the one that missed the ball. So in my experience when we devote our resources fully to creating the conditions, instead of focussing on trying to hit the ball, good shots will come into being effortlessly in their own time.

The Full Swing

I would like you to continue working on the half swing until you feel truly confident in your ability to hit a solid shot with it, since the half swing is a necessary building block for what is to come. In my view very few seasoned golfers ever really come to terms with the action I have just described. By this I mean that they usually hit the ball with an ascending blow and pick it off the surface with a flick of the wrists, rather than hit it with the descending blow of the karate-chop action which takes a small divot after impact. Unless you actually master the correct action no amount of fancy manoeuvres will in any way compensate for your lack of basic technique. This is borne out by the great players, many of whom have weird and wonderful swings, but when their action is analysed they are all rock solid in the impact zone.

So when you can hit the ball solidly with a half swing, it is time to start lengthening it out. I must emphasise that the full swing is an extension of the same factors that we have incorporated into the half swing — a free use of the centre of the body to provide the basic momentum, a coordinated response from the arms that are swinging gorilla- style from the shoulders, and hands used to support the weight of the club rather than actively directing operations.

The difference between the full and the half swing is that we now need to learn to continue winding-up the centre like a spring on the backswing until it reaches its point of greatest tension. In this way we build up power or energy for release on the downswing. Without this strong coiling action we have nothing to unwind at impact and hence can only make a weak swing. In fact most golfers do not wind up their centre sufficiently and instead make what I describe as a 'long' rather than a full swing, with the hands and arms carrying the movement on the backswing by themselves. So our major task now is to extend our vital use of the centre and thus harness the true potential of the swing.

We will begin by learning this movement in slow motion so we can become totally familiar with it in terms of feeling, and then we will tune the movement to the rhythm of our breathing in order to spontaneously release it. As you have already experienced, the centre of the body is our initiating force or engine of the movement. To help you build up an awareness of the desired coiling action I would like you to stop every six inches or so on the backswing in this exercise, and commence each new section with a turn of your centre. You might like to imagine this as a turnstile in action, and make a clicking sound with your tongue as you move into each groove.

Take up your stance and slowly swing back to the halfway point, then stop. Now turn your barrel a little bit more, and hold the position. Feel your legs really supporting you. Next make another little turn of the barrel with the arms reacting. Then just a bit more, and so on until you cannot go any further. This is not a comfortable exercise, in fact the feeling of stretch and strain as we coil the middle of the body can be downright painful in slow motion. You will also feel your legs working overtime to actively carry you, particularly your thigh muscles *(pic 40)*.

Start down slowly with your barrel leading and feel weight moving back onto the flat of the left foot and the inside edge of the right foot. This is simply a more accentuated version of what we have already worked on in the half swing and it brings the arms quite spontaneously into the impact zone. From here your centre starts to slowly turn towards the target, taking more and more weight off the right foot and onto the outside edge and heel of the left foot, and the right arm starts to straighten, fully extending the arc of the swing at impact. Let your head go and allow the turn of your centre to continue into a full finish with your belly facing the target and your hands and head high *(pic 41)*.

As I have already said, this swing only differs from the half

40 A full coil at the top of the backswing.

swing in one major regard, that is the extra coil of the centre on the backswing. All the other features are basically the same with the exception of a longer follow through. The latter is not a matter of conscious choice but merely the result of the extra coiling up of the centre, which means there is more to be unwound on the way down and hence a longer through swing.

I would now like you to repeat the exercise, still working on the coiling action but also taking your attention to your hands and their role of balancing the club. In the early part of the swing the club will feel quite heavy with the left hand supporting the weight of the club. Then as the club moves beyond the horizontal you will feel it getting lighter. As you go further on towards the top of the swing the club seems slightly heavier again, only now the right hand takes some of

41 A poised follow through.

the weight. So what is referred to as the wrist break is not an active breaking of the wrists but the natural yielding of the wrist joints, in response to a combination of the flexing of the right elbow and the pull of gravity as the club gets beyond the vertical. The hands merely do enough to support the club, and nothing more or less *(pic 42)*.

As the centre initiates the downswing the hands are left behind slightly. The wrist break, increased by this yielding of the hands, is retained as we come into the karate chop position. Then you will feel an involuntary tightening of the hands to coincide with the straightening of the right arm in the impact zone. On the way through, the right hand and arm take over and fully extend the arc of the swing, which results in the right hand having the primary role of supporting the club. The left

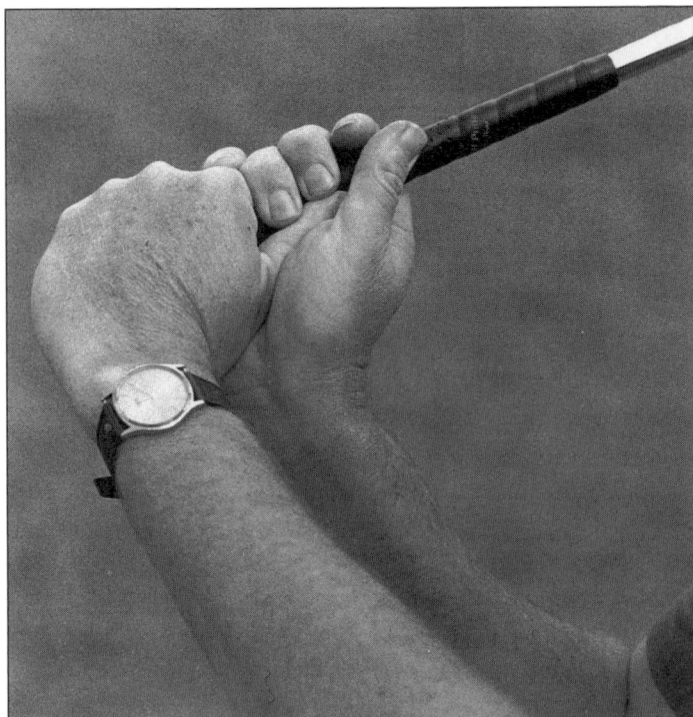

42 The hands are relaxedly but firmly balancing the club at the top of the backswing.

hand and arm yield now just as the right side did on the backswing. Then as the swing continues, tension is released from both hands and we complete the swing with relaxed hands and loose arms. It is as though the tension we built up by coiling the centre on the way back has been completely released or spent.

With regard to the length of the swing, it should be allowed to continue as long as the body is able to coil. If you are short and muscular, for example, you will tend to have a short backswing, whereas tall lanky types, who tend to be more flexible, are able to make a longer one. It is a matter of listening to your body and abiding by the limitations of flexibility within which you have to work. However the stance and swing we have been working on will allow your backswing to find its optimum length because they promote relaxation and therefore increase flexibility.

Our next task is to work up the tempo of the swing from slow-motion to full speed by tuning the movement to the rhythm of our breathing. As before, we will stay in slow-motion until we build up a strong association between the sections of the swing and the pattern of our breathing. As you swing slowly back, breathe in deeply, imagining your barrel filling with air or energy. Continue this inbreath for the full length of the backswing, or in other words for as long as your centre continues to coil. Hold your breath at the start of the downswing as though storing the energy so its release can be concentrated into the impact zone. Then breathe out as your centre turns towards the target, releasing the energy of the swing, and allow the movement to continue into a full and relaxed follow through.

This exercise can be practised with or without a club, in fact you can even practise the breathing pattern in an armchair while clearly picturing the movement in your mind. This is a very powerful exercise because it builds a strong positive image of the sort of swing you want.

Once you have established a relationship between breathing and movement it is time to bring the swing up to normal speed. We do not rush or slow down the swing but in a sense just 'breathe' it, focussing entirely on the rhythm of our breathing, trusting it to release the movement for us. We have prepared ourselves with meticulous care, our body knows what to do, we now need to step aside and allow it to get on with the job.

It is time to introduce that worrisome spherical object, the ball. As we have already seen, the ball presents us with the great temptation of panicking, forgetting everything we have learnt, and rushing headlong into simply trying to hit it. As a result we become tense and totally lose the rhythm of the swing. What is required at this point is an act of faith in ourselves. In this there is no contriving the action, no thought of doing it properly, because that will create a careful and inhibited approach to movement. Instead we have to trust our body, take courage and move in an uninhibited way to the flow of our breathing, simply allowing the clubhead to find its own way to the ball. Thus there is no space between thought and action, only pure spontaneous doing and in this we experience the joy of freedom.

The 'Fundamentals of Good Style'

In contrast to my approach the predominant focus of traditional golf instruction has been the teaching of the so-called 'fundamentals of good style'. However, as we have already seen, it is impossible to externally build qualities into a swing since we cannot self-consciously piece together a complicated collection of mechanical operations in the split second available. Instead, by concentrating our attention on introducing the inward qualities of balance, relaxation and rhythm, we will find that the external fundamentals quite happily take care of themselves. In fact they are not desirable for their own sake at all but merely act as useful indicators of the degree to which we have incorporated our inner qualities. So let us now see how the stance and swing I recommend automatically foster the traditional basics of 'good technique'.

Much traditional advice has centred on the head — for example the instructions to keep the head steady and down. Both pieces of advice are prefaced by the word 'keep'. In my experience, any time we attempt to keep a part of our anatomy still or down, we create tension and destroy freedom of movement. I would go further and say that in the history of golf teaching no one remark has been more destructive than 'Keep your head down', since to artificially do so strangles the flow of the swing. However the head will effortlessly comply with these two well-known pieces of golfing advice when the swing gains a free axis about which to move. We have worked on establishing this axis in two ways: firstly in our stance position, by actively using the hip and knee joints, thus freeing the torso from tension and allowing it to work as our axis; secondly, in the swing we have united both ends of the axis by learning to coordinate the use of the arms and shoulders at one end with a turn of the centre of the body. When these factors come together the swing gains its free axis. In this situation the head, which sits atop our freely rotating axis, has no need to move laterally and so will quite naturally remain steady.

By contrast when the axis is bent and tense, it is impossible to co-ordinate a use of the shoulders and the lower half of the body. The top half thus assumes a dominant role and the lower half gets left behind. The swing then takes on the character of a sway. So what is described as 'lifting the head' is merely the head being forced to move forward with the lateral sway of the body *(pic 43)*.

Another familiar instruction is to keep one's head behind the ball. When the stance is assumed in the way I have suggested, the left arm hangs directly below the left shoulder with the shaft in alignment, thus forming a straight line from the point of the left shoulder to the end of the club. This naturally results in our head starting off behind the ball (see pic 26b), given a roughly normal anatomical make-up! Then by attaching the right hand in the way I have suggested we ensure that the head continues behind the ball. However if we give in to our right-handedness and shift our left hand across to meet the right, our hands move back to the middle of our stance, which results in our head being over the ball.

The swing I recommend also allows us to stay behind the ball since the downswing is initiated in the lower half of the body. The active use of the lower half means that the top half of the body has no reason to take over and automatically stays behind the ball. If the opposite occurs and the downswing is initiated by the hands and arms, the upper half of the body lunges forward, taking the head with it.

Next let us look at the hands, arms and shoulders. Three

43 Here the upper body has lurched forward, taking the head with it. By contrast, good balance naturally leads to the head staying behind the ball — as we see in Pic 1 for example

popular examples of advice in this area are: 'Keep the left arm straight', 'Take the clubhead back low to the ground' and 'Turn the shoulders through an angle of 90 degrees on the backswing'. To explain how my approach naturally aids the emergence of these three traditional instructions, imagine the torso as the axle of a wheel, and the left arm as the spoke of that wheel. When the axle turns freely, the left arm or spoke will remain relatively straight and describe a long, wide arc, and the clubhead will naturally stay low to the ground. I must point out again that rigid straightness of the arm is not what we want, since it will create tension and destroy the rhythmic flow of the swing.

However if the swing loses its free axle due to tension or poor coordination between the shoulders and the centre of the body, movement will be dominated by the hands and arms and the swing will be forced into an up and down chopping action, in which the arc of the swing and the straightness of the left arm are both destroyed (pic 44).

What is called the shoulder turn is in my view not merely a turn of the shoulders, but a rotation of the entire axis. Since we have increased the capacity of the whole axis to turn, by freeing it of tension and by learning how to coil it effectively, we thus allow the shoulders to reach their optimum degree of turn, whatever that might be for each individual.

We now move to the hips and the advice: 'Start the downswing with an active use of the hips'. I agree that the hips, which house the body's strongest muscles, should have an active role in the swing, but I do not think that we should consciously try to use them as this results in a rather dislocated action. In my view the hips will naturally come into play when we encourage their free use, which we have been doing in the following ways: firstly, by removing tension from this area of the body in our posture; secondly by actively using the hip and knee joints to assume a stance, thus improving the flow of movement down into the pelvis; and thirdly by releasing the

44 An up and down chopping action with no pivoting of the body, and a poor carriage of weight in the legs.

centre of the body, thus allowing the hips to turn freely both on the backswing and downswing.

Two other pieces of advice that I feel are related to the use of the hips are: 'Keep the right arm close to the side of the body' and 'Uncock the wrists late in the downswing'. As you will have seen from the slow-motion exercises, when the hips are able to take an active part in the downswing the right arm will quite naturally remain close to the side of the body, and the wrists will only start to uncock in the final phase of the downswing (or karate chop action). In no sense do we contrive this movement. Even if we attempted to do so, the speed at which events occur would make it impossible.

By contrast when the hips do not play an active role, the arms and shoulders will fill the gap and do the majority of the work in the first half of the downswing. As a result the wrists start to uncock early and the right arm comes away from the side of the body.

A final example of traditional advice concerns the need to transfer weight onto the right foot during the backswing and then onto the left foot during the downswing. As you will have noticed from the slow-motion exercises, weight automatically shifts in this way when you release the centre of the body. However this is only possible when we have a stable base from which to work, in other words a stance that effectively uses the hip and knee joints. So when we combine these two factors — a balanced stance and a release of the centre of the body — an active use of the legs and feet will naturally follow and perfect weight distribution will occur.

It is my feeling that the fundamentals of good style came into being through observing what good players looked like from the outside. I hope it is clear from the examples I have given that they will spontaneously occur when we learn what a free swing feels like from the inside. Such a movement can never be constructed, but like a living plant it will blossom of its own accord when we work patiently on creating conditions that foster growth.

4

Common Golfing Problems

IF YOU HAVE A CONSISTENT problem, say topping the ball, you will doubtless have tried to discover a cure. This process will probably have started with the question 'What am I doing wrong?' In the case of topping, the fault is commonly diagnosed as lifting the head and so you will have set about remedying the situation by trying to keep your head down.

As we have already seen the 'keep' instructions only increase the level of tension and further destroy freedom of movement. Moreover this popular approach to curing problems will always fail because it merely supresses the symptoms, rather than treating the cause of the 'disease'.

In order to cure any problem at a fundamental level we need to go a step further and discover what is causing the symptom itself. In my view tension, imbalance and poor coordination lie at the root of all faults, so instead of focussing narrowly on the fault we need to concentrate our attention on restoring the qualities of balance, relaxation and rhythm to our swing. In this way we will cure the problem at its root and the fault itself will spontaneously disappear.

Everybody's swing is a highly individual movement, and it

is therefore impossible to cover all the combinations and permutations that can occur in a golf swing to cause problems. So although you may be afflicted with a problem which we discuss here, it may very well have a slightly different cause to the one I have suggested. However the following examples will give you a method by which you can approach your own situation. In order to avoid copious repetition I will not be going into great detail when it comes to describing solutions to common golfing problems, but rather referring you back to the relevant areas you need to work on, which are covered at length in the Stance and Swing chapters.

The Slice

The slice occurs when we combine an open clubface at impact with a swing arc which slides that open face across the ball (often described as an outside-in swing). This places side spin on the ball and causes it to curve with varying degrees of ferocity to the right. So in order to cure this problem at a fundamental level we need to examine the reasons why the clubhead is open at impact, and what causes the swing arc to be distorted into an outside-in pattern.

Firstly, the vast majority of slicers take up their stance in such a way that their shoulders are pointing well to the left of target. Thus the line of the shoulders is cutting across the line of flight from outside to in, instead of running parallel to it *(pic 45)*. This in turn means that the swing arc will inevitably scribe an outside-in pattern. This common fault in the stance can be traced directly to our need to dominate the situation with the right hand. Any time we move to grasp the club with our right hand our shoulders spin round to the left and we destroy the alignment of the body. By contrast, if you do as I have already suggested and lower the point of the right shoulder with a small see-saw-like tilt of the collar-bone *(see pic 20)*, and then swing the right arm across to meet the club like a pendulum, you will

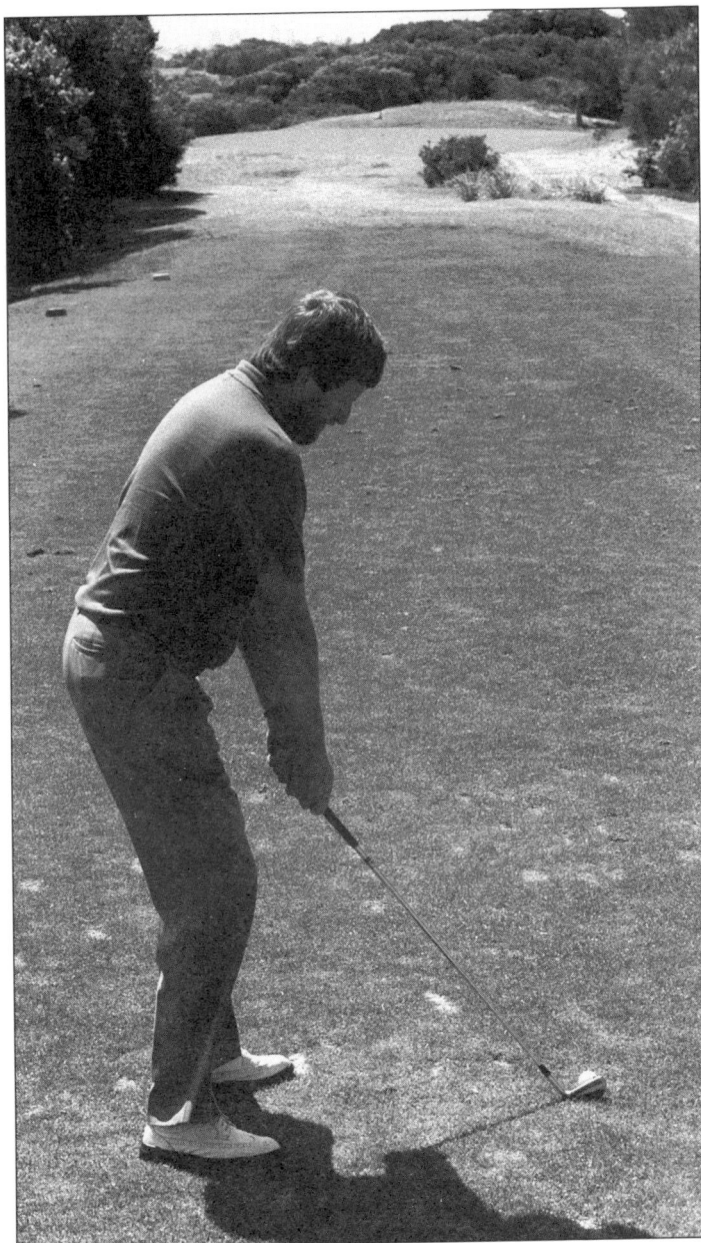

45 The typical slicer's stance, with shoulders well to the left of target.

ensure that the shoulders point in the same direction as the hips and feet, parallel to the line of flight.

The second factor contributing to an outside-in swing pattern is an underuse of the lower half of the body in the swing. This means that the hands, arms and shoulders are forced to do the majority of the work, and instead of being a pivoting turn the swing takes on the character of an up and down chopping action *(see pic 44)*. It is only when the centre of the body makes a strong turn or coil, thus activating the hips, legs and feet, that the swing arc is able to move into an inside-out pattern.

Without the inclusion of the third factor, which is an open clubface at impact, the outside-in swing pattern, rather than slice the ball, would simply hit it straight to the left. This shot is known as the pull, and golfers who do this should not be under any illusions about being hookers of the ball! However when an open clubface is drawn across the ball from outside-in this places considerable side spin on the ball and the full-blown slice comes into its own.

The clubface fans open when our hands take an overactive role in the backswing. Instead of merely balancing the club, which will naturally keep the clubface square, the hands actually swing it which causes the club to open. It is the role of the hands to balance the weight of the clubhead, while the job of providing the major muscular activity needs to be given to the centre of the body.

These three factors are closely intertwined and it is therefore impossible to provide a simplistic solution to such a complex problem. To effectively cure the slice we need to work on many fronts rather than hope for a miracle cure. Slicers will need to begin by improving their stance and body alignment, and then use the slow-motion exercises to develop a swing in which the lower half of the body is actively involved. In addition the hands need to be taught their true role, that of balancing the clubhead, and a way must be prepared for this in the stance by learning to relaxedly fold them about the club rather than grasp it. By patiently working on these points you will find that the problem of slicing is cured at its source.

Topping

Topping occurs when the arc of the swing is shortened in the impact zone making it impossible for the clubhead to get right down to the ball. The problem ranges from missing the ball altogether to thinning it, in other words hitting it in the air but never really collecting it solidly. Many people may not think of themselves as toppers but since they regularly hit the ball thinly they have in fact a 'mild case' of the disease.

What then causes the arc of the swing to be shortened? In my experience golfers who top or thin the ball do so because they try to scoop it up into the air with a flick of the wrists instead of hitting it with a descending blow which would naturally fully extend the arc of the swing. Attempting to lift the ball with this flicking action shortens our arc and makes the top an inevitability *(pic 46)*.

Underlying the problem of topping there is, I feel, a fundamental misconception as to the whole nature of the swing — that in order to hit the ball into the air one needs to get under it and lift it up, hence the scooping action. Paradoxically, to get the ball up, we in fact need to hit down on it. As well as fully extending the arc of the swing and thus getting the clubhead all the way down to the ground, this descending blow puts backspin on the ball, which makes it climb.

So we need to look at ways of replacing a flick or ascending blow with a descending blow. We cannot achieve this by direct means, in other words by making ourselves hit down on the ball. However this type of action spontaneously happens when we use the centre of our body to provide the swing with its major impetus. Initiating the downswing with the centre naturally brings us to the karate-chop position and to the explosive straightening of the right arm which fully extends the

46a A bad case of topping with the back of the left wrist caved in at impact.

46b The correct action. Note the position of the left wrist and also the active use of the legs, particularly the right leg.

arc of the swing at impact. This type of action involves the whole body, calling into full play the hips, legs and feet, while toppers typically rely on just their hands and arms to scoop the ball into the air. So in order to cure the problem at its source we need to work on learning to use the powerful muscles in the centre and lower half of our body to swing the club.

We must begin this process by getting well set on our legs in the stance, so that we have a stable base of support from which to move uninhibitedly. This involves assuming our stance by actively using the hip and knee joints, as I have already described in detail. It is only when we are securely carried on our legs that it is possible to effectively utilise our centre. Next, since we want to fully extend the arc of the swing at impact, we must establish this characteristic in our stance. It is as if we are setting ourselves up in the position to which we want to return at impact. Thus it is important to work on the gravitational hanging of the left arm, and then to re-align the body slightly so that we lower the point of the right shoulder, allowing the right arm to swing across and make a perfect tension-free fit.

As far as swinging the club is concerned I would like you to spend a great deal of time on the slow-motion exercises described earlier, feeling your arms moving from your shoulders in gorilla-like fashion, and coordinating that movement with a turn of the centre of your body. It is most important for the centre to be absolutely coordinated both on the backswing and on the way down. Start by swinging the club back to roughly hip high and feel your weight shift onto your right foot as the centre turns. Your grip should be only just firm enough to support the weight of the club and no more. Then on the way down feel your centre and arms moving slowly together until you arrive at the karate-chop position. Now feel your right arm straighten so that the arc of the swing fully extends itself at impact and continue both the swing of the arms and the turn of the centre of the body until the swing reaches roughly hip high on the follow through.

You will find that this type of swing allows the clubhead to reach the ground easily and take a small divot. In this situation where the clubhead collects the ball with a descending blow, there is no possibility whatsoever of topping it. (This coincides with the well-known golfing advice to 'Hit down and through the ball.')

The more you practise this half swing in slow-motion the more it will become part of you and the easier it will be to do on the course. Then as you gain confidence start to extend the swing, and continue working on the coordinated release of the centre of the body and the swing of the arms. By working in this way you will fundamentally cure the problem of topping.

By contrast, the popular remedy is to advise the afflicted golfer to keep his or her head down. However this approach always fails because it does not address itself to the basic cause of the problem, which is an underuse of the lower half of the body and a domination of the swing by the hands. Trying to keep one's head down actually aggravates the situation because, as we have already seen, attempting to keep any part of our anatomy still or down creates tension and therefore inhibits freedom of movement. In fact I often have to teach pupils to let their head go since artificially keeping it down blocks the forward progress of the swing. To demonstrate what I mean I would like you to try some slow-motion swings and see how it is only possible to fully release the hips and legs when the head is allowed to move spontaneously, and conversely when we keep our head down it is as though the swing hits a barrier that prevents it from flowing through the ball.

So one might say that since keeping one's head down inhibits the use of the lower half of the body it exacerbates the problem of topping rather than curing it! I find I have to encourage toppers not only to let their head go but also indeed to let themselves top the ball. You are better off letting yourself top it than trying not to, because trying always creates tension. By freeing yourself to fail, on the other hand, you defuse the situation and relax slightly thus allowing the body to function more freely, and it is a free flow of movement throughout the whole body right down into the hips, legs and feet which cures the problem. So if you top the ball, let it be a free and glorious top!

The Hook

The hook occurs when a closed clubface is drawn across the ball from inside to out, making it the exact opposite to the slice. The ball starts out heading for the target or even right of target and then curves to the left, in some cases sharp left. The hook is not to be confused with the pull shot which, as we have seen, is a relative of the slice and simply flies straight left.

While we don't want to change the inside-out pattern of the swing arc (since it has the greatest potential for power), we do need to investigate why the clubface is closed at impact.

The first and simplest thing to look at is the alignment of the body. Hookers tend to set themselves up in what is traditionally described as a "closed" position, that is with their shoulders, hips, legs and feet aiming to the right of the target and the clubhead pointing to the target. This means that the clubface is closed relative to the alignment of the body, predisposing us to a hook from the very beginning. The problem is that we are completely unaware how far out of alignment we actually are. In my own game I often feel comfortably set up, yet when I check my alignment to my surprise my feet can be aimed as much as 20 yards to the right of target. Thus it is most important to be scrupulous with one's alignment, because comfort is not a reliable guide.

Secondly, hookers usually have what is described as a strong grip — a left hand that is placed well over the shaft with two or more knuckles visible. To illustrate what I mean let us exaggerate the fault by gripping the club with all five knuckles cleary visible. Then swing back to hip high in slow-motion and notice the hooding effect this grip has on the face of the club.

Now slowly swing down to the ball and see how easy it is for the clubhead to be closed at impact. Players with a strong grip such as Lee Trevino need not necessarily hook the ball but have to work very hard to prevent this premature closing of the clubface. I do not feel that it is ever appropriate to force the left hand into an orthodox position and arbitrarily adopt a one knuckle grip. Rather, we need to discover the way in which our left hand naturally falls from the wrist joint by simply allowing tension to drop away. Then cup the fingers slightly and introduce the club without turning or twisting the hand in any way. This often results in an orthodox one-knuckle grip which will remove any tendency to hood the face of the club. In some cases it will result in a two-knuckle grip because the angle at which the hand hangs varies with each individual. However to force the hand to comply with the dictates of so-called 'correct style' would destroy the free functioning of the wrist joint and create tension in the hands, reducing their capacity to feel. These players will have a natural draw (a slight hook) and will have to tailor their game accordingly. In my view any tendency in this direction will not get out of control unless it is teamed with a slight loss of rhythm — in other words when the centre is not fully released into the shot. The hands then take over a little more quickly than is desirable which has the effect of releasing the clubhead too early, causing it to close prematurely.

Experiment with some slow-motion swings, firstly one in which the centre is released freely into the shot, and notice that any tendency to close the clubface is delayed until after impact. Then inhibit the centre and see how quickly the clubface closes when the hands assume a dominant role. From this experiment you can see how important it is to confidently release the centre into the shot and trust your natural timing to hit the ball. In fact I feel that it is tentativeness, the very opposite of trust, which often lies at the root of hooking. We fear that the hook might get out of control and so we hold back and attempt to steer the ball. Holding back is really holding 'centre', throttling back on the engine of the swing, and when the engine ceases to function effectively our hands take over and fill the void. As with the top, we need to let ourselves go, and hook the ball if necessary, because the freer and more full-blooded the swing becomes, the sooner the hook will turn into a slight natural draw — the sort of shot many of us dream about!

The Shank

There are few shots as devastating as the shank. At its worst it results in the ball flying off at right angles to the intended line of flight. To rub salt into the wound, the shank often comes out of the blue and strikes the unfortunate golfer on what seems like a relatively easy pitch shot about fifty yards out from the green. One minute the prospect of a solid par or maybe a birdie is in view and the next you are hacking it out of the bushes thirty yards to the right of the green. Then when you have hit one shank you spend the rest of the round worrying about it happening again.

As the name suggests, the shank occurs when instead of making contact with the clubface the ball is struck by the shank or hossel of the club. Having been afflicted from time to time by this score-escalating shot I have given some thought to the question of why this happens. In my view it is caused by a combination of the clubhead being fanned open on the backswing, and an inside-out swing arc. This sets us up for the hossel to lead on the way down making the shank an ever-present possibility *(pic 47)*.

While we do not want to tamper with the arc of the swing we do need to understand what causes the shank to be exposed. At the root of this problem I feel there is a degree of tentativeness. We are faced with a delicate shot and instead of trusting the swing to find its own way, we hold back or 'hold centre' and make a tentative backswing. Anytime we hold back even slightly our hands and wrists are apt to dominate, and

47a Here the downswing has been initiated by the upper body, causing the right shoulder to move out and around instead of under. This forces the swing arc to be pushed out into the hossel or shank of the club.

when combined with an inside-out swing arc this causes the wrists to rotate, fanning the clubhead open and exposing the shank. What we need is a much less active use of the hands and wrists in which they merely support the weight of the club rather than directly manipulating it. This kind of action will maintain the alignment of the left arm and clubshaft throughout the backswing, making the shank an impossibility.

So in order to cure the shank it is necessary to teach our

47b Here the lower body, centre and legs have initiated the downswing, allowing the right shoulder to stay back. This will lead to the swing arc coming in to the ball at the correct angle.

hands their role in the swing. To do this I have found the slow-motion exercises essential because slowing the action right down allows us to take stock of what is really happening. Feel the movement inch by inch, allowing your centre to provide the swing with its turn or pivot and use your hands merely to balance or support the club. When the centre and hands are working in unity in this way the clubface naturally stays square to the swing arc. In other words, the clubhead is not being held shut by being taken back straight, but remains in the same relation to the hands and arms as in the stance. Since the swing is a pivoting turn, the clubface appears to be opening on the backswing but it is in fact square relative to the arc of the swing.

Next we need to take courage and trust the rhythm of the body to hit the ball for us. We can only overcome tentativeness and build confidence by letting go and trusting our instincts to hit the ball — not being too careful or trying to be too accurate.

Thus curing the shank is a twofold process. Firstly it is a matter of re-educating the hands so that the clubface remains square to the arc of the swing instead of being fanned open. Then, as I have frequently stressed, we need to let go and trust the body to do what we have just taught it — fearlessly letting the result we want flow from the conditions that we have created.

5

Concentration

IN ORDER TO CREATE our favourable conditions in the first place, and to then make the most of them on the course, we need to master the art of concentration. To concentrate means to be totally immersed in what we are doing at the present time, without thought for anything except the situation that now confronts us. This has been expressed by many golfers as 'playing one shot at a time'.

Most of us, including myself, are very easily diverted from this state of complete involvement. We drift off into other realms and assume (wrongly) that things can be left to take care of themselves. However I am constantly and rather painfully reminded that I need to give my full attention to the task at hand if I am to get the most out of the experience of playing golf, or indeed any other experience.

This poses the question: 'What should I give my full attention to?' In my view there are three areas on which we need to concentrate when we play. The first is a close observation of the conditions that apply on the course, such as the strength and direction of the wind. The second is an acute awareness of what is going on inside ourselves, such as our state of balance when we assume our stance. The last is creatively imagining a realistic solution, in terms of our ability, to the question posed by the shot at hand. Let us now look at these three points in more detail.

The external conditions

We need to observe carefully what the external conditions are saying to us. This means we must take into account the hazards which confront us on the way to the target, make an accurate assessment of our distance to the target on shots in to the green, and notice the direction and strength of the wind, the moisture in the air and in the soil, the way the ball is sitting and the slope of the ground. All these conditions may seem fairly obvious but it is amazing how often we fail to see what is very clearly before our eyes. Since these conditions are always changing we need to be constantly and acutely aware of them, even when playing on exceedingly familiar territory, because the slightest variation in wind can necessitate a change in club selection. A story I heard about Ben Hogan provides an example of this. He was set to play a shot in the US Open one year and just before commencing his backswing noticed a rustling in the trees which indicated to him that the wind had changed direction. As a result he immediately reassessed the situation and changed his club. This is a perfect illustration of total absorption in the present, and acute awareness of the external conditions.

For the most part you will learn how to counter the external conditions through a combination of observation and common sense. However I am so frequently asked for advice in this area that I will give a few illustrations of how to respond to external conditions. If, for example, all the trouble is through the back of the green, it is wise to be conservative in one's club selection and play for the front of the green. When playing in heavy, humid weather the ball will have greater difficulty cutting through the atmosphere so more club is required. If the ball is lying below your feet the tendency is for a fade or small slice to creep in. This is because the slope of the ground causes you to fall forward into the shot a little, bringing the swing arc across the ball from outside to in. In other words the swing will be slightly top heavy. To counter this you need to ensure that a little more weight is carried on your heels, and aim to the left-hand side of the green. The opposite is true when the ball is higher than your feet, and you will need to compensate for a slight hook by aiming to the right of target and reducing your knee bend so that more weight is carried on your toes. When going uphill it is useful to counter the slope by placing a little more weight on your left foot, and the opposite applies when going downhill.

Our ability to judge the distance each club will propel the ball is dependent on us having tuned our swing to the innate rhythm of our body. This is because a rhythmic swing will accelerate the club in an even and predictable way, whereas a jerky movement is irregular in its nature and therefore impossible to predict. So it is only when your swing settles down into a rhythmic pattern that you will be confident in your club selection. This confidence comes from an organic source — in other words, you gain a feeling for the club required — and is not the result of an arbitrary rule which states for example: 'A five iron should go 180 yards.'

The internal conditions

These are our old friends balance, relaxation and rhythm. As we have already seen, these internal conditions can never become habitual, we cannot rely on memory to find them. Rather we need to re-acquaint ourselves with them on each occasion by taking our attention to our body and acutely experiencing our state of balance, allowing ourselves to relax by releasing tension and coordinating our movements by tuning in to the natural rhythm of the body. All these things have to be done in the here and now and require our total concentration. The great temptation is to think that we have 'got' them now, that we have learnt how to balance and relax our body and how to move rhythmically, and then expect ourselves to mechanically reproduce a swing which has these qualities. However, although we may get better at discovering balance, relaxation and rhythm, and may experience them more subtly, we can never cross them off the list as things we can do now and assume they will happen automatically. On the contrary, we need to become ever more intimately aware of them.

Creatively imagining a realistic solution

Our next task is to creatively imagine a solution to the question posed us by the course — a solution which is realistic relative to our ability. By this I mean it is no use working out the ideal shot that Jack Nicklaus would play, because golf is the art of the possible! You need to imagine a shot which you think you can actually play, one with which you feel intuitively happy. This may sound somewhat pessimistic, but on the contrary I feel that to realistically acknowledge one's limitations and play accordingly helps build true confidence, and therefore paves the way for real and sustainable improvement.

So the aim is to work out what we are going to take on. For example, it may not be a 200-yard shot over water to a minuscule green, instead we may elect to play to the left-hand side of the fairway with a five iron and leave ourselves an easy pitch shot to the pin. Having decided what we can reasonably attempt, our next task is to play the shot in our imagination, to practice it in the mind. You can do this on a practice swing by imagining that you are actually hitting the ball — even imagine the sort of feeling on contact, the sound of the ball being struck and the flight which it will take. For instance if you want a light high pitch shot over a bunker which lands softly on the green, feel the rhythm of the swing that is required to hit such a shot, and experience the lightness and delicacy in your body and off the club face that need to be reflected in the shot you are about to play. Then trust yourself, go into the rhythm of your body and allow yourself to play the shot the way you have just imagined it.

I remember watching a television match in which Lee Trevino was taking part. He selected a one iron to play to an elevated windswept green. The putting surface was rock hard so he needed to land the ball very softly. This is no easy task with the extremely straight-faced one iron, but the green was about 220 yards away so a more lofted club would not have reached it. Before playing the stroke, Trevino told the announcer that he was going to play the shot so the ball would land softly 'like a butterfly landing with honey on its feet.' The shot was then played exactly as he had conceived it. Trevino used a very sensuous image to describe the shot he required, providing an evocative suggestion which his body could then translate into action. I am not suggesting you immediately race out and practise honeyed butterfly shots, especially if you are a beginner, but I do feel that in a modest way we can all use our imagination to help solve the problem posed by the course. The external situation is asking a question and we can answer it in our imagination before actually playing the shot, and at the same time give a powerful suggestion to our body as to how to play it.

Diversions

What I have just outlined on concentration will give the mind quite enough to do, and when it is fully engaged, when we are giving our full attention to the task at hand, we become absorbed in what we are doing. It is in this state of being in the moment that our best golf emerges. We can play with clarity of mind and a freedom to act, to execute our shots in a decisive and sure-footed way.

Golf (or perhaps human nature) does, however, offer us a considerable number of possible diversions, ways in which the mind can be seduced away from the total concentration that is necessary. Let us now examine some of these diversions, and then see how to free ourselves from them.

Trying

The most popular diversion from concentration is trying. This may surprise you because most of us think that trying and concentration mean the same thing, but they are fundamentally different. In my view, trying revolves around using the will to make the body do what we want it to do, whereas true concentration seeks to elicit the body's cooperation. The latter requires us to be fully present in the moment, perceiving with great sensitivity what is actually happening and fashioning a solution which feels right for us now. When we 'try', on the other hand, we always have a fixed idea in mind of how the swing 'should' be. So rather than being open to what the present has to tell us, we are trapped in a struggle to impose an old pattern upon it. Let us now look in detail at some well known examples of trying.

Trying to implement the 'basics of good technique'

When we try to implement the so-called 'basics of good technique' we are attempting to impose on the body a preconceived pattern. The mind is thus used to send the body a series of instructions about how it should operate in order to copy the pattern properly. The famous 'keep' instructions are a good example — keep your left arm straight, head down, eye on the ball, etc. In trying to follow these directions the mind takes on the role of a sergeant major barking a stream of orders at a rather unwilling body.

In attempting to carry out all these instructions in the split second available we naturally become apprehensive or fearful lest we mess something up. This creates tension, which only increases our chances of failing. The problem is usually compounded because in the face of failure most of us redouble our efforts, in line with the saying 'If at first you don't succeed, try, try, and try again.' However I can assure you from painful experience that this only makes things worse because the harder you try the more tense you become and the more likely it is that you will fail. This will either lead you to give up the game out of a mistaken belief that it is impossible or turn it into a long frustrating battle.

When we are truly concentrating the mind is used to perceive the body sensitively, so rather than being an admonishing, dictatorial figure it becomes a good listener. In this way the mind and body can work together to create conditions that are conducive to the best possible outcome. For example, in order to arrive at a balanced stance position, we must give our whole attention to our state of equilibrium. We need to listen to or feel the messages that are coming back from our feet and make fine adjustments until we arrive at a stable position. We cannot 'try' to balance our body, all we can do is tune in and trust that we will learn to distinguish fine differences as our perception improves. This kind of approach cannot be turned into a pattern which we try to remember and copy, rather we have to re-experience it afresh on each occasion.

Trying to hit a good shot

Trying to hit a good shot includes trying to hit a long drive or an accurate shot, say a drive down a narrow fairway or an iron shot to a small, heavily bunkered green. In the case of trying to hit a long drive, we are using conscious effort in a vain attempt to add power to the swing. Yet we all know that our most powerful shots seem to magically appear out of an effortless swing. However this does not seem to stop us from being lured into thinking that the expenditure of ever increasing amounts of effort will enable us to hit the ball still further. When we do this we push the swing beyond the body's natural rhythm and inevitably mess up the shot.

It is clear that we cannot arrive at a powerful drive by

direct means, in other words by willfully trying to achieve our ends. Rather, by concentrating on bringing into being our old friends, the qualities of balance, relaxation and rhythm, we will find that we are able to tap into a natural source of power.

Trying to hit an accurate shot may seem different because rather than increasing the power in the swing we are holding back. However in holding back we are still consciously controlling the swing and not letting it flow freely. This has often been described as trying to steer the ball, and its effect is just as destructive as trying to hit the ball powerfully.

Why do we hold back on a shot? This can occur when we doubt our capacity to successfully carry out the assignment we have given ourselves and we become tentative. We may feel that we have taken on too much but think we 'ought' to be able to play the difficult shot. In my view we need to listen to our doubts and not try to override them because they are often giving us accurate information on the most appropriate way to act. So if you are not happy about playing a shot, think again and pick one which you do feel you are able to handle. In this way you will feel confident about the result, which goes a long way to improving your chances of success.

As we increasingly get in touch with our body it is possible to become more daring in the shots we take on because we instinctively feel more confident about our capacity to successfully carry out difficult assignments. I must emphasise, though, that it is no use being daring or careful as a matter of policy, we need to learn to trust what we intuitively feel is right for us at this moment. In some cases it might feel right to be bold; in others, a more defensive path seems the best.

Obsession with the score

I am all too familiar with this diversion because I have spent much of my golfing life working out in mid-round how well I was going. For example after nine holes I might be two over par and have a short putt for a birdie on the tenth, and instead of giving myself fully to the situation my mind would be chattering away with 'If I get this one I'll only be one over.' The situation gets worse as the round progresses, especially if one is going reasonably well and has a good chance of breaking one's handicap or playing one's best-ever round — all the way up to having a one-shot lead with nine holes to go in the US Open. In short, all golfers are subject to this type of thinking. Their orientation towards the result takes resources away from the means whereby the result can be attained. In other words, if our mind is fully engaged in preparing the body for movement and creatively imagining the shot best suited to the situation, then we are completely absorbed in this task and will have no mental space for worrying about the score. For example when Gary Player last won the British Open he had been in the unusual position of more or less leading the tournament from the first hole. By the time he got to about the seventh hole in the final round he had built up a substantial five-shot lead. At this point he turned to his caddy and said 'How am I going?', to which his caddy, Rabbit Dwyer, replied, 'I'll tell you after you've played the seventeenth hole.' Two or three holes later Player said: 'Have we got to the seventeenth yet?' He was so engrossed in his inner world that he had totally lost touch with the number of holes played and had no idea of his score.

We can also become obsessive about the par of the hole, seeing it as the score we 'should' get. Yet par is a purely arbitrary figure which takes no account of the prevailing conditions, not to mention our varying abilities! I remember playing a par 5 hole into such a strong wind that three perfectly hit wood shots and a wedge were required to reach the green. Then on a hole of similar length but down-wind, just one drive and a nine iron saw me safely on the green. So one might say that par is absolutely irrelevant, it is what you can do on the hole right now that counts.

Good shots and bad shots

Good shots and bad shots have an equal capacity to divert us from concentration. If we have just hit a perfect shot there is a strong temptation to want to repeat it by reproducing the swing that we have just made. We are diverted from the present because we are trying to hold onto the past. In order to do this we may seize on one aspect of the previous swing, say a slow deliberate take away, which we identify as the magic secret. We then set about implementing this secret, using the conscious mind to tell the body what to do — in other words we try to do it properly. Because of this the swing becomes highly mechanical and we lose the very freedom and spontaneity that were so characteristic of the perfect shot. The words of William Blake illustrate this point beautifully:

> *He who binds to himself a joy*
> *Does the winged life destroy;*
> *But he who kisses the joy as it flies*
> *Lives in eternity's sun rise.*

Bad shots have the capacity to divert us, because like good shots they send us scurrying off into the past, this time to work out what we have just done wrong. We then sort through our collection of old hoary golf tips in the vain hope that we will hit upon a miracle cure. This may even work for a short time since we all have an unreasoning belief in the power of the magic potion and this temporarily relaxes the mind, but if you are anything like me you will have found that miracle cures all end in disappointment.

This whole approach to problem solving fails because it is centred in the past — firstly worrying about what we have just done wrong and secondly dredging up an old potion. We are thus diverted from bringing our attention to the only area in which we can productively operate, and that is the present. Whether it was good or bad, the more we can simply let our previous shot go, the better. In this way we release our full energy for a fresh start on the next shot and thus maximise the chances of a free swing emerging.

Wanting to improve

A similar problem to good and bad shots is struggling to improve, only in this case we are focussed on what we want to be. So instead of drifting into the past we are diverted into the future. We want to arrive at our goal so much that it becomes an obsessional pursuit and we become frustrated and despondent when we fail to make progress.

It seems paradoxical, but in order to improve we have to relinquish the need for improvement and accept things the way they are now. This is not to say that we are powerless, but improvement or growth comes in its own time. We therefore need to gain the capacity to wait patiently without expectations. In a sense all we can do is gain a greater subtlety of perception with regard to our body and mind, a realistic appreciation without criticism of our strengths and weaknesses, and a keen observation of the external conditions. When we concentrate our attention on these things improvement will occur naturally in its own time as a matter of course.

Fear of failure

We unfortunately live in a society which worships success and so its opposite, failure, becomes something to be feared. This fear of failure creates tension because we brace ourselves against the result we fear, which only increases the chances of failing. For example if we consistently slice the ball, the slice becomes a symbol of failure and we get into the position of fighting it so hard that all our resources are diverted into the struggle to avoid what we fear. The harder we struggle against our fears the more power they have over us. In my view, rather than fighting our fears, we need to extend to ourselves the freedom to fail. I have found it helpful to use one of Louise Hay's affirmations — 'It's OK to make mistakes while learning' —

immediately after hitting a bad shot. By allowing ourselves the luxury of failure it ceases to be such a threat and its power over us begins to disperse.

At every stage of the game we need to give ourselves this latitude to make mistakes. For example if a pupil is topping the ball in a lesson, I encourage them to let themselves top it. This always has the effect of relaxing the pupil which in turn helps to cure the problem. At the other end of the scale, the legendary Walter Hagen used to allow himself seven bad shots per round. In this way a mistake was not seen as a threat but as a human error that needed to be expected and accepted.

Once we are no longer fighting our fear of making errors it then becomes easier to concentrate our full resources on creating conditions which are most conducive to a favourable result.

Other people

Most of us are easily diverted by other people simply because we often concern ourselves with what they may be thinking of us. For instance, as we take up our stance in a disciplined way we may fear that other people are thinking: 'What is this idiot doing carrying on with this performance? Who does he think he is, Jack Nicklaus?' Then we worry about messing up the shot itself, since we fear we will look an even bigger fool if an abortive shot comes at the end of lengthy preparation. Yet any time we concern ourselves with what other people may be thinking we are not giving our full attention to the task at hand.

In order to detach ourselves from this all-too-popular diversion we need to understand why we are apt to worry about what other people think of us. In my view it stems from the fact that most of us depend upon the approval of others in order to feel good about ourselves. When we get positive feedback we feel affirmed, and in the face of criticism we feel somewhat threatened. In this situation we are constantly worried about the opinion of others since their estimation of us determines how we see ourselves. With such an attitude we can never give our full attention to the task at hand, let alone be free and spontaneous.

The cure for this problem is to learn to accept and value ourselves unconditionally the way we are now, no matter how bad that might be. It is no use waiting until we are perfect to make a start on this important project, because we will be waiting for ever. We therefore have no choice but to take courage, make a bold statement about who we are now, and to hell with what other people might think of us. It is only when we have truly accepted ourselves, warts and all, that we can be fundamentally free from any concern about the opinion of others. Then and only then can we bring our full attention to bear on the situation which now confronts us.

The belief that we have no talent

Many of us have been so conditioned to think of ourselves as innately useless in some areas that we feel there is no chance of us ever learning anything new. It is as though we have been taught to lack confidence in ourselves. Believing that we have no talent prevents us from concentrating because we cannot be bothered giving our full attention to what we are doing, it feels like a waste of time. Why indeed give our energy to something, why venture at all, when deep down we feel that it is all hopeless? Needless to say, with this attitude we are defeated before we start.

I find this problem haunts women golfers in particular, probably because women have been encouraged to have low self-esteem, often as a result of being undermined by the all-knowing males in their lives! However anyone whose talent does not lie on the surface can be forgiven for believing that it does not exist at all. The task here is to bring something forth that is not visible at the present time. This requires an act of faith, we have to take courage and admit the possibility of being able to play one day. You can, for example, practise imagining yourself as you would like to be, or simply say to yourself 'I can learn.' After all at one stage we were not able to ride a bicycle, but we were able to learn to. We did not come out of the womb riding a bike but we did come equipped with the ability to learn new things.

Once you have taken that brave step and acknowledged the possibility of progress, you can begin to gather your resources in earnest. If on the other hand you choose to cling to the belief that you have no talent you commit a kind of psychological suicide by absolving yourself of the responsibility of drawing something out from within. It is like burying your talent in the ground rather than accepting the pain and frustration inherent in any voyage of discovery. In my experience we may indeed have to dig deep to find what we are looking for, but it is only through venturing that we will find it.

Resisting the work of concentration

I feel in myself and from my experience of teaching that there is some underlying resistance in all of us to the level of total involvement required in concentration. It is as though there is a power of inertia to be overcome. We find it difficult to give ourselves fully, to feel intimately and prepare ourselves with care time and again, shot after shot, to work and keep on working. But to give ourselves fully to the moment is also an exhilarating and ultimately rewarding experience, because in so doing we lose our old constraining boundaries and gain a new sense of freedom. With such rich rewards in store why is it that we hold back?

In part, I feel, it is because concentration involves letting go of our mental habits in order to plunge into the present. It is certainly easier not to bother. However I suspect the underlying reason for holding back is that we fear giving up our addiction to the 'trying' mode — we want to stay in conscious control of what we do since this allows us to feel secure. To this end we seek out fixed formulas to cling onto, hence the popularity of golf tips. What I am asking involves relinquishing this attitude entirely, since awareness and sensitivity call for a completely receptive state of mind. In this we have no preconceived pattern to follow, no prescription to implement, instead we are thrown on our own resources, and have to learn to place our trust in what is after all a rather intangible area of ourselves — our feelings. This degree of vulnerablility may feel uncomfortable at first since we are exploring what is for many people a new dimension. However in order to explore it we have no choice but to overcome our longing for security and give ourselves fully to an acute awareness of ourselves. In the same way, learning to swim involves letting go of the side of the pool and pushing off into the deep.

The 'Cure' for Diversions

I do not think that we will be able to cure ourselves of diversions by repressing them. So it is no good saying 'I shouldn't feel inadequate or puffed up or obsessive about results', or giving ourselves a metaphorical slap on the hand each time we stray into these areas of thought. Rather, we need to become more aware of what we are doing to ourselves. Once we are able to clearly see our habits of thinking their power to divert us is already diminished, because it is only the patterns of which we are unconscious that really have us in their grip. So our task is one of acknowledging what is actually happening, often just below the surface. This involves us in a fascinating study in that we are getting to know ourselves more fully.

As we begin to see our behaviour for what it is we will hopefully gain the capacity to laugh at ourselves, and not with scorn but with affection. I feel that the cure for diversions lives in this area of honest acceptance without criticism or excuse. In this situation we are neither ignorant of our faults nor fighting against them, but are learning to recognise them. With practice we are able to see them earlier and earlier and let them go before we are thoroughly ensnared. For example, I can see in myself that my mind very easily wanders into 'What did I do wrong?' thinking after a bad shot. I am now able to catch myself in the act and let that thought go before it has done too much damage.

As our destructive thought patterns drop away we are increasingly able to give our full attention to the task at hand. In a sense we take our thoughts inward into feeling instead of having the mind chattering away with irrelevant and unhelpful detail. In a true state of concentration we are totally at one with ourselves. There is no separation between mind and body, no part of us issuing orders or criticising: rather we become the swing itself. Here thought and action merge into one, and we experience exhilaration and freedom.

6

Putting
&
Other
Shots

LEARNING TO PLAY GOLF is not a matter of acquiring a collection of disparate skills for each separate situation. Every aspect of the game can be seen as an integral part of the whole, since the same underlying principles apply all the way from the tiniest tap-in through to the longest drive. Let us begin on the green and work our way out to the tee.

Putting

It has often been suggested of putting in particular that it is a game within a game, but I regard it as a miniature version of the swing on which we have been working. It is, however, the area of the game which requires the greatest degree of subtlety — one might describe it as the fine needlework at the end of the hole. In order to putt well we need a smooth, even stroke and a highly developed sense of touch or feeling, combined with acute judgement of pace and direction. I feel the best way of enhancing smoothness, sensitivity and judgement is to introduce into our putting our old friends balance, relaxation and rhythm.

As with all other shots, we will need to begin by assuming our stance in a balanced way. The importance of stability may not be immediately obvious to you since the stroke itself is short and does not therefore greatly strain the body's ability to maintain itself in a state of equilibrium. However the delicate and precise nature of the stroke makes it especially vulnerable to any unstabilising oscillations that inevitably occur unless we are perfectly balanced. So it is just as vital to be securely balanced over a putt as it is on any other shot. Also if you play, as I do, on coastal links you will need all the stability you can muster to secure yourself against the buffeting of the wind!

Relaxation is important in putting as in other shots, in that it aids sensitivity of touch by allowing us to feel more acutely what our body is doing and by giving us a heightened sensation of contact with the ball. The more tension we are holding the less feedback we receive from our body and the less aware we are of fine differences of sensation as we strike the ball. In addition, relaxed hands, arms and shoulders allow us to swing the club freely and hence smoothly, whereas tension in these areas makes for a jerky unreliable stroke.

Rhythm is essential because it enables our movements to flow together. When our putting stroke has an even, rhythmic flow we have a sound basis around which to make judgements, since the predictable nature of our movements aids decision making. On the other hand a disjointed jerky unrhythmical stroke has an irregular pattern, and thus we are without a reliable basis for good judgement.

It is in this area of rhythm that my approach to putting differs radically from much traditional advice. In my view our movements will never be truly rhythmic without the participation of the lower half of the body, because by definition rhythm is a flow of movement throughout the whole body. It is therefore impossible to freeze this vital area out of the movement (as is advocated by much teaching) and still have a rhythmic stroke. Since a putting stroke is by its nature very short I am by no means suggesting a wildly exaggerated use of the pelvic muscles but a subtle flow of movement into the lower half of the body.

The putting stance

I would now like you to take up a putting stance in exactly the same way as I have suggested you do for a normal shot, by folding the body concertina-style at the hip and knee joints so that the weight of the body is securely carried on the legs. It may seem strange at first to stand so erect over a putt since the most common approach is to hunch low over the ball, but as we have already seen it is impossible to swing rhythmically from a collapsed position.

Our next task is to establish the free-hanging point of the left arm by allowing it to fall like a length of rope from the shoulder with the hand hanging relaxedly from the wrist joint. This may sound easy but we need to consciously give our complete attention to imagining the arm relaxing, so that it really lets go and hangs where gravity dictates. I am inclined to unconsciously pull my arm in towards my body, and am often surprised how far away it falls when I let it hang naturally. So it is absolutely necessary to rediscover this free hanging point each time we assume our stance because it is impossible to remember where the arm 'should' hang. The right hand is then used to place the club in the cupped fingers of the left hand. Next we make a small see-saw like tilt of the collar-bone so that the right shoulder drops slightly, allowing us to swing the right hand across to meet the club, forming a perfect tension-free fit *(pic 48)*.

So as you can see we stand and hold a putter in basically the same way as we do for any other club, albeit with a narrower stance. This has the advantage of removing the need to learn a completely new stance routine. One final remark: the putting grip needs to be very gentle as we will not be using our hands to wield the putter but to acutely perceive fine differences, in other words to sensitively feel. Our hands cannot fulfil this function if they are squeezing the club to death!

The swing

Having set the body up for free movement our next task is to explore the nature of a rhythmic putting stroke. As I said earlier, a putt is a miniature version of the swing on which we have already been working — a dance of the whole body from the fingertips to the toes. Since it is impossible to learn such a movement by mechanical means (in other words by forcing the body to comply with a set of instructions), we have to learn it from the inside, using slow-motion exercises to acquaint ourselves with the feeling of a rhythmic stroke. Then, as with the full swing, we will be learning to use our imagination to help us release ourselves spontaneously into the movement.

Firstly I would like you to assume a putting stance with a club and allow your arms to slowly swing gorilla-fashion a short way back and forth. At the same time imagine the centre of your body releasing with the swing and notice the subtle shift of weight which occurs even in this small slow movement — very slightly onto the right foot on the backswing and through onto the left at the end of the swing. I must stress that we are imagining or allowing the centre to release and not consciously trying to make things happen, so it is not a marked transfer of weight but a subtle change of emphasis in response to the natural flow throughout the whole body. Also notice how this rhythmic movement allows the putter to swing smoothly and evenly, as though it is swinging itself.

I would now like you to repeat the exercise but this time hold the centre of your body rigid. With the lower half of your body frozen completely out of the action in this way, notice how uptight you feel (you may find yourself unconsciously holding your breath) and how the swing loses its smooth, even flow. In fact it ceases to be a swing at all and becomes a taking

48 The angular, relaxed putting stance I recommend.

of the club back and forth. Finally release your centre once again and feel your arms moving freely. Rather than taking or controlling the putter, you will again feel that it is truly swinging or finding its own way.

From the preceding exercise it will be clear that smoothness and evenness in a putting stroke revolve around a coordinated use of the whole body, in other words around that vital quality, rhythm. Let us now do some more slow-motion swings but this time focus our attention on our hands. They should only be doing just enough to support the weight of the putter, since in this way they will be as relaxed as possible and thus able to sensitively perceive fine differences of feeling when we come to strike the ball. This is vitally important in putting because sensitivity is one of the crucial factors in the development of good judgement.

Next take up a putting stance without a ball. Lift the club a fraction off the ground, holding it just firmly enough to support the weight of the head. Then allow this weighty object to swing very slowly pendulum-style back and forth, allowing your wrists to hinge slightly, and feel the evenness of pressure in your hands as the movement takes place. The wrists are not consciously broken, neither are they held out of the movement, but rather allowed to hinge naturally as the putterhead swings back and forth.

Still in slow-motion I would like you to experiment with under-using and then over-using the hands. Firstly hold your wrists rigidly out of the movement, prevent them from hingeing at all. Notice how tense this makes your hands, arms and shoulders. You will feel that you are taking the club back and forth rather than swinging it. Needless to say that in this situation the hands lose most of their sensitivity because they are tense and the stroke loses its free flow or rhythm. Then allow your wrists to hinge freely once again and see how effortless and natural the movement feels.

Now go to the opposite extreme and, still in slow-motion, make the entire stroke with the hands and wrists, holding the rest of the body out of the movement. Notice how tense your hands feel and how the stroke loses its evenness and becomes wobbly and irregular, with the clubhead lifting high off the ground and fanning open. It feels like agonisingly hard work particularly if you move ultra-slowly, as though the putter is a weighty object you are struggling to move. To conclude, re-integrate into the stroke a swing of your arms and a release of the centre and see how smooth and easy the movement feels.

In addition notice that when your hands are not used to direct operations the putterhead naturally complies with the traditional advice and stays reasonably close to the ground and square to the target line.

I hope you have gained an awareness from these slow-motion exercises of what a good putting stroke feels like. You will need to return to these exercises frequently because we are dealing with a sensitivity to feelings which can only be renewed and refined through practice. Needless to say, by practice I do not mean mindless repetition but a taking of our whole attention to the qualities of balance, relaxation and rhythm.

We are now ready to bring our stroke up to normal speed and to introduce a ball and target. When we come to hit the ball we need to assume our stance in a highly disciplined way and then use our imagination to spontaneously release ourselves into the movement, trusting that our body now knows what to do. Let us start with a practice swing. Take up your stance, giving your full attention to your body's state of balance, the relaxed hanging of your arms, and to the gentle balancing of the club in your hands. Remember your hands are used in the first instance merely to support the weight of the club and not to wield it.

As with the full swing, we now need to attune our stroke to the rhythm of our body and once again we are going to use our breathing to help us do this. I want you to think of nothing else but tuning the movement to your natural rhythm of breathing. So as the putter swings back feel air or energy flowing in right down to your stomach, and time contact with an imaginary ball to coincide with your outbreath. I must emphasise that you should not consciously force your breathing but allow it to flow naturally. If we breathe deeply in this way the centre will release in time to the swing of the arms and the whole body will flow together spontaneously.

Now introduce a target and vividly imagine the stroke required. Really see the line you want the ball to take and the way it runs across the turf. The beginner will have to venture a guess and discover how it works out in practice. In fact it is a guess for all of us, but in time it becomes a more educated one. Then, as before, tune the stroke to the rhythm of your breathing and see the imaginary ball run towards the target.

I used to think it was a waste of time imaginatively conceiving what I wanted. Now I realise that the more immersed I am in using my imagination the freer I am to act. I am not saying this provides a magic solution, because we also need to gain an acute bodily awareness, but I do feel that this approach helps to free us from the fear and doubt created by trying to do it properly.

Now introduce the ball. With the image of what you want clearly in your mind let yourself do exactly what you have just imagined, breathing in on the backswing and out as you make contact, releasing the ball to find its own way to the target. It is important not to try to make the ball go in the hole, rather prepare yourself both physically and mentally and then allow yourself to hit it. In this way our attention is always focussed on creating conditions and not on trying to gain our ends by direct means.

At this point we need to explore the final ingredient necessary for good putting, that of judgement of pace and direction. I am often asked 'How much stroke should I use to get the ball to the hole?' Since the rhythmic stroke we have been working on accelerates the clubhead evenly, the longer the stroke we make the more time it has to build up speed and the further it will propel the ball. Conversely the shorter the stroke, the slower and shorter the putt. However we cannot stand over each putt mathematically working out the exact length of stroke required as that would lead to a paralysingly self-conscious and inhibited movement! Rather we have to build up an instinctive knowledge of how much stroke is needed. We do this by learning to associate the feelings of hardness or softness produced at contact by varying lengths of stroke. (By the way, since a rhythmic stroke utilises the strong pelvic muscles it does not need to be overly long, and you will find yourself propelling the ball much further than usual with a relatively short stroke. This has the advantage of reducing the overall size of the movement and thus increasing its reliability.)

You will need to experiment with differing lengths of stroke and really focus on the feelings they produce in your hands — hence the importance of relaxed hands that are able to perceive fine differences. As we become increasingly conscious of the feelings which come back to us from the clubhead on striking the ball we develop an awareness of the relationship between length of stroke, hardness of hit and the resulting putt. Gradually, through practice, you will come to instinctively know the length of stroke required.

It is then a matter of placing your trust in this intuitive judgement, but most of us interfere with this to some extent. For example I am sure that, like me, you have had the experience of knowing you have left a putt short the instant after striking it. In this situation a part of us knows what to do but we hold back and inhibit the free flow of the stroke. In my view the only way we can overcome this common problem and build confidence in our instinctive judgement is to free ourselves to exercise it on every possible occasion. We can only learn by venturing — by letting go of our need to get it right and trusting that our 'failures' have much to teach us.

Thus far we have seen that good judgement rests on both a connectedness with the rhythm of our body (which provides a predictable pattern of acceleration) and an acute awareness of feelings in our hands. However since greens vary enormously we must also become sensitive to what the external factors are telling us, in other words we need to learn how to read the green. This revolves around keen observation — noticing the slope, thickness and moisture of the turf and the grain of the grass (the direction in which the grass grows). For example if the ball has to battle its way into the grain it will be slowed down considerably. Even the wind can have an effect. On an exposed green, for instance, one may have to aim to compensate for the prevailing wind. These factors are in themselves very simple, but the problem many of us have is taking the trouble to notice them. It is easier not to bother. Yet accurate observation is vitally necessary because it is impossible to make sound judgements around limited information.

Having seen the importance of the internal and external factors in judgement we now need to actively bring these two together in order to answer the question posed by the green. I do this by making a practice stroke and clearly imagining the feeling of the club making contact with the ball and watching it run towards the target. It is only when I feel intuitively happy and settled about the imagined putt (some players describe this as 'getting set') that I actually hit the ball.

I hope you have seen that in essence a putt is no different to any other shot, merely a more delicate and precise version of a longer swing. As with the full swing, careful preparation is of paramount importance while the stroke itself needs to be free and spontaneous. Any attempt to directly control the stroke will destroy our natural rhythm and spontaneity. This is not to say that discipline has no place, but it belongs in our detailed preparation. Our body is willing and able to move as we want it to, but we need to use an intelligent and logical approach in order to have it work effectively and thus draw out our natural potential.

I regret ending these thoughts on putting in a negative vein but before we move on to other shots it will be helpful by way of contrast to look briefly at what most people do when they putt. The most common stance is a hunched affair with bent arms which hug the body (pic 49). The lower half of the body is rigidly excluded from the movement and so the stroke itself is dominated by the hands. The 'keep' instructions have a field day in putting — not only has the head to be kept down but the whole body is treated like a restless child and ordered to keep still!

49 The all-too-popular hunched over, cramped putting stance.

At its best this type of stroke can be reasonably fluid since the wrists are at least free to hinge. However it has severe limtitations. Firstly it is very difficult to maintain a consistent arc to the swing because in essence there is no swing at all — by which I mean there is no swing of the arms from the shoulders, but merely a flick of the wrists which at worst can become jerky and unpredictable (often described as the 'yips'). Secondly, with the lower half of the body immobilised we are unable to tap into our natural rhythm. Also since the hands are burdened with the majority of the work they become tense and therefore have a greatly reduced capacity to perceive fine differences of feeling as we strike the ball. When we are out of touch with our bodily feelings in this way we naturally become tentative, because we have nothing real on which to base our judgements. It is drawbacks such as these which to my mind make this common approach to putting completely untenable.

The Chip and Run

This little shot is played from just off the green, when the terrain to be covered is relatively flat. I usually use a 7 iron and think in terms of lifting the ball just over the fringe and running it up to the flag. One might even see it as a long putt, with the first part of the journey just above ground. In fact we can simply adapt a putting action, albeit with a slightly longer stroke, using a 7 iron. Our stance needs to be relatively narrow, about the same as for a putt, and slightly open, by which I mean the hips and shoulders are pointing to the left of the target. This helps to get the body out of the way, allowing freedom of passage for the arms on the throughswing *(pic 50)*.

The chief misconception with regard to the swing itself is that the lower half of the body should be kept fairly still. As we have already seen, rigidity in the hips and legs will result in a poorly balanced, top-heavy action which lacks rhythm and delicacy. Yet the chip, like all shots at this 'fine needlework' end of the game, depends on delicacy of touch. So we actually need a movement initiated in the centre of the body that integrates the hips and legs, leaving the hands free to feel. With regard to the subtleties of judgement, a chip is very similar to a putt in many ways. Varying lengths of shot require a shorter or fuller swing and we have to rely on what feels right to guide us in this area. Only through venturing will this sense of what to do develop.

50 The stance for chipping.

The Pitch

The pitch shot is used when we want to carry the ball high over an obstacle, say a bunker, and land it softly on the green. It is generally played with a wedge or sand iron, using a slightly open and fairly narrow stance — about half shoulder width. The common misconception here is that we need to get under the ball and lift it up in the air with a flick of the wrists. However we actually need to be hitting the ball with a descending blow and taking a divot after impact. This type of action automatically puts backspin on the ball which both makes it climb and causes it to stop quickly on hitting the green. This descending blow will quite naturally happen if we use the centre of our body as the engine of the swing. Try this out for yourself. Hold your centre out on a swing and see how it is impossible to take a divot. Then use the centre and experience the ease with which the clubhead cuts through the grass. So playing a short pitch shot really gets down to gaining the confidence to let the centre flow and trusting that the club will find the ball automatically.

With regard to judgement of distance, the fuller the swing the further it will propel the ball. However a longer swing is not a matter of taking the arms further back but of using an increased turn of the axle to tell the arms how far to go. Then on the downswing the club has more time to build up acceleration, sending the ball further. We do not tack on a longer throughswing either but simply allow the movement to continue until it runs out of momentum.

I mentioned earlier the possibility of using a sand iron, which has the advantage of hitting the ball higher in the air and thus having it land more softly and stop a little more quickly. Generally speaking though, because of the rounded sole on a sand iron, we need a relatively good lie to attempt this shot. Whichever club we choose, these high floaty shots depend on a confidently rhythmic swing because there is little margin for error at this precise end of the game. The more we can practise letting go and trusting, the better will be the result.

The Bunker Shot

The bunker shot is very similar to the pitch, the only difference being that insted of hitting the ball first we start our divot before the ball. This gives a cushion of sand between the clubface and the ball, allowing us to lift it out of the bunker and land it on the green very softly. The stance again is open, with the feet aiming to the left of target, and the clubface pointing at the target *(pic 51a)*. This allows us to cut across the ball slightly and gives us a somewhat more upright swing so we can get right down into and through the sand. The bunker shot revolves around exploding the ball out with the sand, and a flat swing does not do this *(pic 51b)*.

Most people get into trouble with the bunker shot because they do not follow through, they chop at the sand rather than swinging the club through it. The action we want will quite naturally occur when we use our centre well, because in using the centre well what I described earlier as the karate chop automatically happens. This results in the clubhead going down and through the sand, which is precisely what we need when in a bunker.

It is also necessary in a bunker shot to aim the club for an inch behind the ball *(pic 51c)*. However the rules of golf do not allow us to touch the sand while assuming our stance so we need to have the clubhead hovering just above the point where we want it to descend. One other thing which can be useful, as an aid to balance, is to wriggle our feet into the sand so we have a secure footing. This will make it easier to move confidently and decisively.

Once we have perfected the karate chop action described above we will lose all fear of the bunker shot. This also helps make our approach shots more confident since we lose that feeling of impending doom at the prospect of finishing up in a sand trap!

Iron Shots

We have already seen in detail how to play an iron shot in the chapter on the swing. Although there are many different clubs to choose from, at all times we are dealing with the same basic

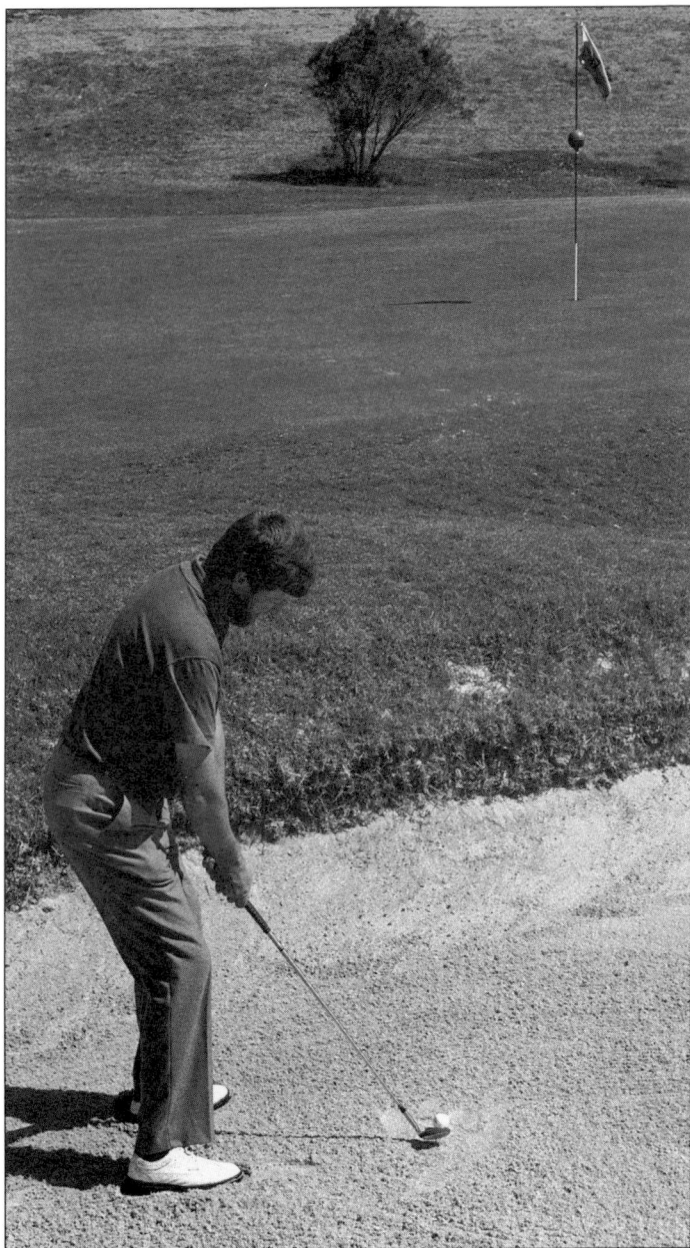

51a The stance for a bunker shot.

51b The bunker shot explodes the ball out of the sand.

51c Here I have replaced the ball after hitting the shot, in order to show the crater in the sand following a good bunker shot. A lot of sand will be exploded out in the correct action.

action. In fact the only thing that varies in iron shots is our distance from the ball — the shorter the club, the closer we are to the ball and vice versa. I must emphasise that our arms are not pushed further away from the body to accommodate a long iron, nor does our body angle change in any way. On the contrary, the clubs are designed to allow us to take up exactly the same stance but at varying distances from the ball *(pic 52)*. Our feet need to be shoulder width apart in all iron shots.

For reasons of simplicity I play all my iron shots with the ball about an inch inside my left heel so my hands are slightly ahead of the ball to start with *(pic 53)*. This means the ball is struck before the swing reaches the bottom of its arc, placing backspin on the ball, which both allows it to climb high in the air and

52 The design of the iron clubs allows the body angle of our stance to remain exactly the same, all that varies is our distance from the ball.

to stop quickly on reaching the green. At the same time I must add here that it is not the end of the world if we are in error to some extent in the finer points of ball placement! So long as the fundamentals of balance, relaxation and rhythm are sound we will not come really unstuck. Golfers in my experience tend to get obsessed with the fine print and lose the main plot.

With regard to the swing, the same rhythm is used throughout, all the way from a delicate 9 iron to a full-blooded 2 iron. The temptation is, however, to force the longer irons. The mind cannot fully believe that an effortlessly rhythmic swing will do the trick and so we are seduced into trying to hit the ball harder. This creates tension, throws us off balance and completely wrecks the rhythm of the swing. So we need to work on slowing down and taking it easy as we move into the longer irons.

Now comes the question of which iron to choose. I am not keen on detailed charts which tell you exactly how far from the green you are, and then a process of mathematically working out what club you should be able to use. Rather, we need to gain a feeling for what is the right shot and this will vary from person to person and from day to day, depending on whether we feel ready to climb Mount Everest or as weak as a kitten. To help me work out what to do I try all the possibilities in my imagination and eliminate what does not feel right. Then I test this out in practice, realising that there is no great disaster in store if I am wrong. By this process you will in time build up faith in your natural judgement. After all, when driving a car we are not constantly instructed on what speed to take a corner, but come to know instinctively what the right thing to do is. I see too many people agonising over-seriously about what to do on a golf course, as though the fate of nations depended on it. What we need is to freely venture, knowing that we can learn from all mistakes. In this way we can come to trust the subtleties of our internal judgement.

53 Ball placement for iron shots.

54a

Wood Shots

Let us start with the wood shot off a tee, which might be a 1, 2 or 3 wood. I only use my driver or 1 wood when I am feeling confident and warmed up. By that I mean I do not race onto the first tee without practice, pull out a 1 wood and expect to hit a good shot. I would be more inclined to use a 3 wood for the first few tee shots and gradually work my way up. If I feel particularly rusty I might even consider an iron shot. The first hole at my course is easily reachable, with two 5 irons.

In comparison to an iron shot the stance for a wood is slightly more upright, with less release of the joints *(pic 54)*.

54b There is a subtle difference between these two positions – the stance for a wood shot (54a) is slightly more upright than that for an iron (54b)

This is because woods are considerably longer so we do not need to be as low to the ground. This is only a slight difference, the basic principles of the stance are exactly the same. Since we need maximum stability it is advisable to have our feet slightly wider than shoulder width. However this is just a personal preference, so experiment and see what works best for you.

With a tee shot the ball is placed opposite the instep of the left foot *(pic 55)*. In this position the clubhead has reached the bottom of its swing arc and may be even on the way up slightly at impact. This is important with a straightfaced club like a driver since it would be impossible to flight the ball with a

55 The ball placement for tee shots.

downward chopping action. As for the height of the tee, I like to get a third or a quarter of the ball protruding over the top edge of the inlay, which is the inset in the middle of the clubhead. For those using a metal wood however, I have found it better to tee the ball a bit lower unless you specifically want to hit a very high, soaring shot say down wind. This is because metal woods have a lower centre of gravity and so make it easier to get the ball up in the air.

As for the swing, it is exactly the same as for all other full shots. I must stress that rhythm is particularly important since any attempt to force the swing will have a disastrous effect. (The longer the shaft of a club, the longer the arc of the swing and the more any error in the swing is accentuated.) The temptation to use effort and therefore lose rhythm is greatest with the driver. As with long irons, it is as though we cannot really believe that an easy rhythmic swing can produce power. Yet we all know that our best shots come from an effortless swing. It is not a matter of self-consciously slowing down, but of letting go and trusting the innate rhythm of our body.

With fairway wood shots the only thing that changes is the ball placement, which moves a little further back, about opposite the heel of the left foot. This means that the clubhead will neither be descending as it hits the ball nor slightly on the way up but will be reaching the ball at the very bottom of the swing arc. We want to be just brushing the grass with the club as it swings through.

It is possible, especially with the introduction of metal woods, to use the driver or 1 wood off the ground and in effect have an extra fairway wood. The ball needs to be sitting very well and one's confidence riding high in order to attempt this. As with all clubs it is a matter of experimenting and seeing what feels right for you. Some golfers are naturally more at home with iron shots and so the 1 iron is a useful addition to their armoury, while other players feel that for them woods are much easier to hit and so some long irons are discarded and replaced by lofted fairway woods.

I would like to emphasise, by way of conclusion to this chapter, that the secret of enjoyable golf will never be found merely in the acquisition of more golfing equipment. Yet hardly a week goes by without the release of some new 'miracle' of golfing technology which claims to revolutionise the game of even the most humble practitioner. In my opinion we are basically being sold the illusion that the answer really does lie outside ourselves. It would be a disaster of the greatest consequence if this illusion were indeed true because the game could then proceed on an entirely materialistic level and we would completely miss the opportunity to find a solution within ourselves — an altogether more interesting, satisfying and fruitful place to conduct our search.

7

The

Journey

Of

Learning

IT WILL BE CLEAR by now that this whole method of learning
hinges upon us making a radical change in our approach to the
game, from one in which we have by and large memorised and
implemented external technique, to one in which we move
towards a growing awareness of ourselves, body and mind.
Many people may find , as I have, that this change in direction
takes them into unfamiliar territory since our experience of
learning has rarely required us to seek a solution within
ourselves. In order to help and encourage you along this new
path, I would like to share with you certain aspects of the
journey as well as some of the problems which inevitably have
to be faced on the way. In my experience each and every
difficulty, far from being a stumbling block, contains within it
material of immense value to us from which we can learn a
great deal, and thus continue our journey with increased
confidence.

One of the basic facts we need to accept is that this method
will not yield us instant results. The growth of our awareness,
whether it be physical or psychological, does not come

overnight. It takes time and energy to perceive even something as simple as an increased feeling for the quality of balance, or to become really connected with the centre of our body from which we have become estranged through lack of use. So we have to learn perseverance, patiently allowing new perceptions to emerge in their own time. I have often described this as a process of osmosis — you let things seep in bit by bit and do not try to force the result. In fact the more you can say to yourself 'I will work patiently and let the result come in its own time' the better, and conversely the more you fight and try to produce a result the more frustrated you become. One might see this as a rhythm of learning, letting things flow and not using effort to force the pace.

After all, awareness, like the growth of any living thing, is in the final analysis out of our control and cannot be forced into existence. We can give our full attention to an area (indeed we must in order to nurture growth) but we cannot make insight happen. New awareness always seems to break through of its own accord, often when we least expect it. Since we like to think that we are in control and can in a direct way achieve the result we want when we want it, we will not always find it easy to be receptive and simply wait. However, wait we must if something new is to emerge, and by 'new' I mean a fundamental shift in our perception or awareness and not the rearrangement of what we already know.

Yet in no sense are we passive victims, waiting for lightning to strike, so to speak. On the contrary we have to be extremely active participants in the process because we can receive insight only if we are ready and alert. This requires of us that we continually make the disciplined effort to notice and respond to what is actually happening now. This is activity of a subtle and inward-turning nature, but it is none the less very demanding work. It is also work which must be done alone since no-one else can take on awareness for us. While someone else can tell you about relaxation, for example, only you in the end can discover what this living quality really is, by directly experiencing it. In the same way, only you can introduce balance and rhythm into your game, only you can focus your attention and only you can find a solution to the questions asked by the course. It is in this sense that we must take full responsibility for our own situation.

Thus in working with this method we need to strike a balance between the passive and active elements in the learning process — waiting and trusting on the one hand and disciplined preparation on the other. If we err on the side of passivity and don't take on awareness we are not grounded in reality, we simply don't know what is going on and it is unlikely that change can occur. If, however, we are not prepared to wait for insight to come, if we demand instant results and use our will to try and make everything happen now, we crowd out the space needed to receive new awareness.

I am reminded here of an anecdote from the north of England, about a gardener who had created a beautiful garden. The local minister was strolling past and remarked on the glory of God's work manifest in the garden. To this the gardener drily replied 'It may well be God's work, but you should have seen it when he was doing it by himself!' In a sense both these characters have a point. As with making a garden, we must at the same time work hard on creating ideal conditions for growth and also acknowledge that there is a dimension beyond our control, and have the patience to wait.

Another characteristic of learning through awareness is that it is a continuing process. We never get to a point of arrival after which we can retire, put our feet up and presume that things can be left to take care of themselves. To be aware, we need to constantly tune in to the reality of the moment, since there is always something new to notice right now and yesterday's experiences are as nothing until rediscovered afresh today. If we take the quality of balance as a simple example, it is not enough to have known balance last week or even on our previous shot, we have to experience that living quality now. Certainly we can get quicker at recognising when we are slightly off, but the minute we slip into automatic and presume that we have 'got it', we are no longer tuned in, we are out of touch with the reality of our state of balance and error creeps in behind our back. So like it or not we are involved in an ongoing process because awareness by its nature has no end.

At first you may find the prospect of this unending process of self-awareness, requiring you to work for the rest of your life, somewhat daunting. I suspect it arouses a degree of resistance in most of us. After all this view of learning runs counter to a deeply ingrained expectation in our society which is that the goal of learning is to 'get there', to arrive at a point of final resolution. From there on we hope to have 'got it all together', all our problems will have been completely sorted out and nothing will really rock us again. In other words we want to reach a point of invulnerability and so retire from the process of learning altogether.

This myth is such an integral part of our conditioning that it may be operating in us on a very subtle level. Even though we may not be fully conscious of its presence this attitude seriously hinders the learning process; in fact for me it has been the greatest single barrier to growth. When we are trying to 'get there' we are struggling to reach an ideal of how we want to be, we have a target in the future for which we strive. This makes us unaccepting and critical of the way we are now because we are always comparing where we are now with where we want to be or where we have fleetingly been. When our state of mind is one of comparison and dissatisfaction we are not receiving or valuing what this moment has to offer and so it is unlikely that our awareness will expand and bear fruit. One might even regard it as a recipe for frustration in that we are blocking what we could be discovering now.

It seems paradoxical, but if we can abandon the hope of getting there and simply work in the moment, value the moment in all its aspects, the more we can receive what the moment has to offer and the more we can learn from it. When our attitude is one of accepting and valuing what the present can give us, our awareness can expand and lead us to the riches that are available now.

So rather than seeing the goal of learning or mastery of the game in terms of 'getting there' — putting an end to the process by arriving at a state of invulnerability — I see it in terms of being ever more at one with the process, being more and more alive to every moment, receiving and working with it in all its facets. Thus the myth of arrival which appeared in the beginning to offer security, in fact cuts us off from the source of growth, and the ongoing process, which started out as a rather daunting prospect, actually brings us life.

One problem we will encounter along the way is the sheer difficulty of accepting and valuing what each moment has to offer when the going gets rough. It seems easy to be at one with the process when things are going well but we tend to become despondent when we strike a bad patch. I think most of us would like to just hold on to the highs and annihilate the lows. Yet golf is very much a game of fluctuating fortunes in that no matter what our standard of play we all experience ups and downs. In fact flux is an inevitable part of all life — everything from the weather and the economy to the state of our feelings is ever-changing. Only something mechanical never changes, so to expect absolute consistency from ourselves or our swing is a denial of the fluctuating nature of life.

Thus it is futile resisting or fighting the down-turns in our game just as it is bewailing changes in the weather. We must, however, go further than grudging acceptance and come to see our bad patches as a valuable part of the learning process rather than as a nuisance to be endured. It is our difficulties which indicate what we need to attend to and it is by working through these areas that progress is made. Once we realise this our problems become helpful signposts telling us in which direction to turn our attention. By contrast, if we were protected from all challenges in an error-free paradise we would never learn anything new.

Unfortunately in the face of our difficulties most of us do not have such a positive approach. Some people get depressed while others strike out in anger and frustration. I for one have been guilty of smashing the odd club in rage. Understandable though these reactions are they do not provide a conducive atmosphere for learning since we are too caught up in our emotions to gain much insight. In a sense our real problem is not so much the original difficulty (such as a persistent slice), but rather the negative response it triggers in us. If we can calm the emotional turbulence we can start to see the original problem as a signpost and follow it through to a successful conclusion.

So how can we change our attitude from one of resisting and fighting our bad patches to one of listening to what they have to tell us? Firstly it is helpful to understand how we acquired our negative attitudes in the first place. I suspect that as children we were never taught to value error, in fact we were punished and made to feel inferior and stupid if we made mistakes. Approval was given only to those who got the answers right. This taught us to be afraid of error, to dislike our imperfections and made us reluctant to admit them to ourselves, let alone others. It is easy to see how we came to value ourselves only when we were free from error and thus developed a basically negative response to our difficulties.

We are not, however, victims of our past, we have the capacity to change these patterns of thought. The first and most fundamental step we must make is to fully acknowledge what we are feeling and thinking day to day, especially when the going gets rough. Only such rigorous honesty will show us what we are up against. Simply observe yourself as objectively as possible, almost as though you are another person watching yourself, and admit what is actually going on. You may notice for example that you regularly put yourself down, like someone I know who used to call himself 'dope brain' after each bad shot, or you may find you feel depressed or angry when things don't go the way you would like them to. As well as noticing your feelings and thoughts it is essential to also observe your reactions to them. By this I mean become aware of both your original feelings and how you feel about them. Are you, for example, critical of your tendency to be self-critical? Do you simply hate all your uncomfortable feelings and want to be rid of them? These are certainly common responses, but they keep us locked into the very cycle of negative attitudes which we need to break.

This vital process of self-observation can be greatly aided by keeping a notebook in which you jot down your reactions to the situations you find yourself in. Such a journal is useful in alerting us to the unconscious patterns that have established themselves in our behaviour. The more we can bring these patterns into the light of day and see them for what they are, the easier it will be to change them. This is very important work because we cannot move to a positive attitude until we have acknowledged the negativity which has ensnared us. It is of no use superimposing optimism on top of unconscious negative attitudes any more than it would be building a new house on rotting foundations.

Having taken some steps along the road of self-awareness we are then ready to make the key move which will break the cycle of negativity surrounding error. In my view the only way to do this is to unconditionally love and accept what we see in ourselves no matter what that might be. In so doing we extend to ourselves the freedom to be wrong and unresolved. While it is easy to love our strengths it will take some time and patience to come to love our weaknesses, but there is no alternative if we genuinely want to get off a destructive treadmill and on to a self-nurturing path. Just as we would cleanse and bandage a physical wound rather than beat it with a stick, so we need to give up beating ourselves for our faults and imperfections and start to tend them with love and understanding.

In practical terms, how do we make this change of direction? We can keep a check on our state of mind by asking ourselves a direct question such as: 'Am I comparing myself to how I think I should be, or am I accepting and nurturing myself as I am right now?' If we discover we are on a negative path we can then use some simple affirmations or truthful sayings — something like 'I will stick with myself through thick and thin', 'I am not against myself, I am for myself' or 'I'm OK just as I am right now'. I have found such sayings really helpful, they provide something to hold on to when the going gets tough. You might like to make up some of our own, anything will do so long as it affirms your worth.

This is not a once-off move, we continually have to both observe ourselves and make the shift to a positive course. However as we gradually learn to love ourselves through the bad patches, the emotional turbulence surrounding error starts to clear and we are able to gain some distance or objectivity as far as the original problem is concerned. In this state of improved clarity we can listen to what the bad patch is telling us. For example if we have been consistently slicing the ball we can read this as an indication to work on strengthening the use of the lower half of our body. Similarly any tension we discover in ourselves, whether physical or psychological, gives us the opportunity to let it go. Without the tension to guide us we could never reach a deeper level of relaxation. In the same way an awareness of imbalance points us in the direction of finer balance. Once we recognise that it is error which leads us to truth or understanding, we begin to welcome all mistakes as a chance to expand. In my case, instead of bad shots provoking a deflated 'Oh no!', I now say to myself 'Let's see what I can learn from this.'

Thus our change of attitude is finally cemented in place by

following through on our problems and finding that they do indeed lead us to new insight and growth. We can now face difficult patches with increased equanimity since we realise that we can benefit from everything that comes our way. In fact it now becomes clear that each moment in the process is either a perfect moment to be enjoyed or a perfect lesson from which to learn.

Gradually as we experience our ability to learn from everything that happens we will find that real confidence begins to grow in us. I must admit here to some reluctance to use the word 'confidence' at all since it has acquired so many negative connotations. I certainly do not mean a brash inflated view of our own competence, nor an exercise in mental gymnastics where we try to think positively in spite of evidence to the contrary. Rather it is a growing trust that if we play our part something will creatively emerge out of whatever situation we find ourselves in. One might describe it as a faith in growth as our natural birthright. Far from being a personal possession for which we take credit, confidence is a gift which we need to receive with thanks since it is drawn from the nature of life itself.

The part we play in the development of confidence is self-awareness, since it is awareness which brings us into touch with the ever-changing reality of the moment. Only this direct relationship with reality opens us to life and growth. If we are unaware, we are out of touch with the real state of affairs and closed to what life is trying to tell us. In this situation any feeling of confidence is, to say the least, on shaky foundations.

Since none of us are in a state of total awareness we continually need to be working on narrowing the gap between what we think is so and what truly is. This work requires humility. We must be humble enough to see and accept the truth of our situation, because in seeing things as they actually are we move closer to reality and to confidence. So, far from being opposites, as is popularly thought, humility and confidence are inextricably linked.

Being open to life in this way means admitting all our experience, including doubt. This can be difficult because we tend to fear our doubts and see them as the antithesis of confidence. In fact doubts are vital clues which are trying to break through and be heard. By listening to and working through them we are brought more into touch with reality. However we often want things to be right so much that we are not honest with ourselves. We have doubts niggling away in the background but try to mentally override them. As a simple example, we may think that we have performed the hip and knee release perfectly and therefore should be balanced. Yet our body may be telling us that it feels vaguely insecure. Rather than seeing these doubts as a threat or a nuisance we need to recognise their usefulness and respond to them. Like a tightrope walker, we have to know when we are slightly off-balance and make corrections. If we fail to listen to these promptings we inevitably mess up the shot, and probably utter the remark 'I knew I was going to hit a bad shot.' The more we can listen to and act upon our doubts the more we strengthen the root system of confidence.

However there is one kind of doubt that we should question, and that is paralysing self-doubt, feelings of inadequacy, and the thought 'I can't do it'. Understandable though these feelings are at times, if we allow ourselves to be taken in by them they will hold the stage unchallenged and seriously undermine the process of learning. What we need to realise is that unlike our previous examples, chronic self-doubt does not give us accurate information about the real state of affairs, but is largely the product of our negative conditioning, — what we have been taught to think about ourselves. This is not to say that we should repress our self-doubt or lurch into Pollyanna optimism, but rather acknowledge its presence and then question the truth of its message. We can also nurture ourselves through times of overwhelming self-doubt by reminding ourselves of a deeper level of truth about life, which is that we are born to grow.

In addition I have found it helpful to realise that self-doubt often comes up at times of change, when we are moving away from what we know and venturing into new and unexplored territory. For example we may well experience some uncertainty as we relinquish the security of a prescriptive method of learning and increasingly take responsibility for our own situation. Once we understand that the appearance of such doubts is a natural part of progress we will feel less threatened and more accepting of them. In this way, rather than seeing doubt as a sign of weakness we can come to recognise it as a harbinger of growth.

By now it will be clear that confidence is not the cocoon of apparent certainty that we thought it was, nor does it lie in the exclusion of those feelings which appear to be its opposite. Rather it is an attitude of mind, an openness to all life and a trust that by venturing ourselves we will learn and grow.

Finally, before we leave the journey of learning let us explore what we mean by success. Is it to find the perfect golf swing, attain a single-figure handicap or maybe even win the US Open? While it might be pleasing to reach one of these goals, there is I feel a much more satisfying and lasting form of success available to each of us all the time when we are working with awareness. It lies in being at one with ourselves, unconditionally accepting who and where we are right now, whatever our standard of play might be. When we come to such a point of complete acceptance, we are released from the struggle to be other than we are and experience a sense of success and joy in simply being ourselves.

As we live in a highly competitive society this may seem a rather unusual view of success. It does not depend for example, on other people seeing us as successful, nor on winning in competition with others, nor even on improving our own game. Our sense of success is independent of all these things once we accept and value ourselves as we are. Paradoxically, in releasing ourselves from the need for external results we create an ideal psychological climate for improvement, in that we are no longer pressuring ourselves to achieve and are therefore free to venture and to learn.

Since many of us have long equated success with ambitious striving to achieve a goal, the suggestion that it rests in being at one with ourselves as we are now may sound like either passive resignation or a recipe for smug self-satisfaction. In fact the exact opposite is true. It takes both hard work and humility to drop the need to be different and to continually see and accept ourselves as we really are, warts and all. Far from being an easy way out, the discovery of inner success is actually a highly active process requiring us to make a radical change in attitude. Instead of habitually resisting how we are now and hoping for fulfilment in the future ('I'll be happy when I break 80' for example), we begin to find our fulfilment in the present, choosing to see the way we are, with all its difficulties and imperfections, as good enough.

In these terms, success is something we can all participate in, it is not restricted to the celebrated few. Nor is it limited to the high points in life, it encompasses the whole of our ordinary experience including our so-called mistakes and failures. Instead of involving a struggle for perfection, it means forgiving our imperfections and taking into the fold everything we find ourselves to be. So rather than being a future achievement which we hope will redeem us, success is here all the time waiting for us to discover it.

How then in practical terms do we make the change of attitude necessary to experience success? We have already made a start on this process in many ways, in particular by letting go of the need to get there, and by changing our attitude to error. There remains one highly destructive habit which we must recognise and relinquish — that of comparing ourselves to other people. Comparison prevents us from finding a sense of inner success because it always takes us in the wrong direction, away from unconditional acceptance and into evaluating ourselves with reference to others. When we compare ourselves unfavourably, for example, we soon start feeling that we are not good enough as we are, we simply don't 'measure up'. Here comparison has the effect of undermining our feelings of worth. At other times we use comparison to boost ourselves up by looking down on those whom we regard as inferior in some way. Here it cannot be said that we unconditionally accept ourselves either, since we depend on putting other people down in order to feel good about ourselves. Whichever way we use comparison, and we all use both, it invariably signals a turning away from our central task, which is to accept and value our own journey.

Golf provides us with ample opportunities to observe comparison at work, all the way from the handicap system to unspoken 'longest drive off the tee' contests. In fact comparison is such a pervasive and deeply ingrained habit that it will take some time to become aware of it and to break away. There is, however, a powerful tool which can help to free us, and that is the fact of our uniqueness. Comparison becomes meaningless once we realise that each and every one of us is a completely unique individual and therefore literally incomparable. We need only look as far as nature for evidence of this often-forgotten truth. Everything in nature, each leaf and each snowflake for example, is known to be unique in itself, and so are we in every aspect, from our fingerprints to the idiosyncracies of our golf swing. When we really grasp this idea of our essential uniqueness we can use it to help put comparison aside. For instance repeating an affirmation such as 'I am unique', each time we catch ourselves in the act of comparison, will remind us of the truth and point us back in the right direction.

In withdrawing from all comparison we create in effect a

haven of self-acceptance, a place where we are no longer resisting how we are nor desiring to be different. Here we are at one with ourselves and can work with and appreciate the unique nature of our own journey. Here we find the freedom and spontaneity which transform an ordinary game of golf into a stimulating and satisfying experience. Here we can enjoy and give thanks for simply being who we are. This to my mind is true success.

I hope in the previous pages to have helped enrich your experience of playing golf. When we learn through awareness we are liberated from the constraint and conformity of traditional technique and can instead work on creating the physical and psychological conditions which best foster freedom.

In addition I hope to have placed the game in a broader context so it can be seen as a medium for discovering about ourselves and about life. One might regard a golf course as a verdant playground in which we are free to experiment and to learn. Viewed in this way the game becomes a pleasurable adventure in self-discovery which can enhance our whole life.

Index